CHASING PIG'S EARS

EARS

(Memoirs of a Hollywood Plastic Surgeon)

John Williams, M.D. FACS

Trafford rev. 02/19/2021

 www.trafford.com
North America & international
toll-free: 844-688-6899 (USA & Canada)
fax: 812 355 4082

Foreword

BEING A TWIN is a gift of nature. From the beginning a twin has someone to share life with. Most sets of twins are very close. A few are competitive. We were not. Jim and I were like two horses pulling the same wagon. It was great. We had the good fortune of having twin sisters who were ten years older than we were. We learned a lot from them. They were so identical that sometimes even our mother had a hard time telling them apart. The girls had a good time being twins. They often went on dates together and occasionally when returning from the restrooms switch dates and the guys would never know it. The only bad part is when one twin gets married and the other one doesn't, as in our case, it is quite an adjustment for the single one because he is alone for the first time in his life. This memoir is about Jim also since our lives were, for the most part, the same. Not quite like Siamese twins but close.

Jim inherited the engineering skills like our older brother, Bill. They both had the natural ability and creativity to invent or improve on most any mechanical problem they came across. They could make precise drawing to scale. To mention a few: a complicated tool to cut diamonds to scale, a boat that was unsinkable, a stretcher that swiveled in the middle allowing a patient to be removed from an airplane or a narrow, steep stairway. Jim designed a way to cap the oil well fires set by the Iraqis in Kuwait. He designed the best liposuction cannulas for removing unwanted fat from patients. He designed a small head strap for his Poodles to keep their ears out of the dish when they were eating. He named it "Pretty Ears".

Bill became the head of the experimental tooling division of Douglas Aircraft and specialized in tooling that required the use of compound angles. Jim went on to medical school with me but looking back even though he made a fine surgeon he probably could have become very wealthy if he had formed a company to make and sell his inventions. This was true also of Bill because all they needed was some business partner who knew how to market their products.

Table Of Contents

Acknowledgement

THANK YOU TO my son, John Christopher Williams, for his help in putting this book together. I also want to thank all my ex-wives for allowing me to tell the truth.

A Note To The Reader

THE OLD CLICHÉ "you can't make a silk purse out of a sow's ear" is true in most cases but once in a while, we in plastic surgery get lucky and come fairly close to pulling it off. We try not to promise the patient more than we can deliver so it's a narrow margin. The most rewarding outcome is a happy patient who got more improvement than was expected. There are those who are basically unattractive (I hate the unkind word "ugly" but that's what they are). I'm referring to the person that has poor bone structure, terrible skin, and an imbalance to their facial features.

The trend toward improving our techniques in the past few years include the correction of all layers (skin, fat, fascia, muscle, cartilage, tendon, and even bone), has improved our batting averages considerably. Also high tech equipment such as the Endoscope, Laser, Ultrasound liposculpting, the surgical microscope and the use of synthetic materials has contributed to our successes. We can now grow tissue and even body parts in the lab.

In spite of all the improvements, we still have one little challenge that exemplifies our search for perfection. When a lesion (mole, tumor, etc.) is excised, it usually leaves a round defect. In closing this wound from a circle to a straight line (surgical scars are most often a straight line), leaves excess tissue at each end that is often referred to as pig's ears (or dog ears). In order to create a smooth closure of the wound, these troublesome little fellows require excision, which further lengthen the wound, and merely leave a lesser pig's ear. If this is continued, one will soon have a scar that runs across the entire face or around the body. We call this "Chasing Pig's Ears."

Introduction

IN "TINSEL TOWN," as Hollywood is often referred to, a youthful appearance is critical, especially among those in "The Business." As a result, Hollywood (Beverly Hills / Los Angeles) has become the Cosmetic Surgery Capital of the world, with the possible exception of New York City. There are more facelifts, breast implants, nose jobs, liposuction and Laser peels done in the Los Angeles area than any other place on earth. This has made it very attractive to young surgeons who aspire to become "Plastic Surgeon to the Stars." Some of these are good and some are not. When it comes to evaluating a surgeon here, it doesn't seem to matter what kind of results he's produced but instead what celebrity he's done. "If famous people go to him he must be good" Is the rational.

There was in fact a very successful plastic surgeon that built his practice on a bad nose job. It didn't seem to matter that after six operations it no longer looked like a nose but instead a pinched bit of skin in the middle of a face, camouflaged by makeup and a curlicue of hair hanging over one eye. It didn't seem to matter that there was obstructed breathing. It only mattered that it looked a little more like Diana Ross' nose.

The surgeon that did the first "conservative nose job" was a professor at UCLA. A young resident in training there at the time got to know the patient and as he was finishing his residency and setting up his practice he took this famous patient with him. Since the patient wanted a much smaller nose he talked the doctors into doing not one but somewhere between two and six more times.

The main characteristic of most African American noses is the thick skin especially on the tip. Each time additional surgery was done there was increased scaring and contracture until the skin became a shapeless deformity. This was not a Rhinoplasty for a beginner, but strangely enough it didn't matter. This was the beginning of a great practice with a stream of the famous and not so famous patients unmatched in the history of the specialty. "He must be the best if this major celebrity chose him, so that's where I want to go." Only in Hollywood!

The fortunate part of this story is this young surgeon ultimately turned out to be a competent surgeon. He learned his craft by trial and error, as we all did. The only difference is that it took great courage and sizable balls to do it on such a famous face. However, luck was with him since one of his first patients in his new private practice was Michael Jackson. He couldn't lose.

In considering just how a novice learns these very delicate techniques of surgery it becomes clear that there is a dilemma. The young doctor has to start somewhere to make the transition from textbook to the operating room. It's a big jump from reading about how to do an operation to the actual surgical experience of cutting into and making changes in the living tissue of a human body. The old adage of "see one, do one, teach one" is a joke but it happens. Many times the clinical instructor doesn't have much interest in teaching or even the expertise in doing the surgery much less in teaching. He shows up the morning of the scheduled operation but only hangs around in the coffee room in case the resident gets into trouble and calls him in. The obvious fact is that in order to really teach, one has to be "scrubbed in" at the operating table so that in a split second he can prevent mistakes.

On some occasions even that might not be quick enough to prevent a disaster. The young doctor already thinks he knows enough to be on his own and doesn't really need the attending physician and if the attending is not at the operating table, where he should be, it shows that he really doesn't care.

I was scrubbed in while attending on a breast augmentation being done by the chief resident at UCLA. This particular young doctor prided himself on being a fast operator. While preparing a space under the pectoralis muscle for placement of the saline filled silicone implant, he entered the lung cavity. It happened so quickly that no one could have prevented it. When this occurs air is sucked into the chest cavity, the lung collapses and the patient has difficulty breathing. The anesthetist with his endotracheal tube in place has a closed system and is able to re-expand the lung after the hole is closed, if it is possible to close it. If not it requires the placement of an intercostal tube (a tube inserted between the ribs and into the chest cavity) with a water seal in order to keep the lung from remaining collapsed. If ever there was a place where "hands on training" is needed it is in the operating room.

On the morning of February 21, 1997, there was a segment on Good Morning America about "how people could have cheap cosmetic surgery if they are willing to have it performed by resident doctors in training." I can see this as an inexpensive way to have a hair cut, but surgery? The whole idea of student surgeons is one of the gray areas in the medico-legal climate of today. Young doctors can't lean without willing patients but if something goes wrong who is at fault? The university has some type of blanket insurance to cover mal practice claims but I have never been informed as to how liable the attending physician really is.

It always amuses me when I hear someone say that they want a young surgeon to do their operation because conventional wisdom tell them that since he has just finished his training that he must be current with the latest techniques. This implies that the older surgeon has not kept up with the latest advances and improvement in techniques and technology. This may be true in a few cases but a surgeon like this was probably not a very good surgeon anyway. The theory that the young guy would be better is a "fool's concept." Even if he is totally current on the latest information, he has not had time nor experiences enough to apply his new knowledge very well. He has not yet developed his skills and, even more importantly, his surgical judgment. One of the most revealing questions one should ask a young surgeon is, "how many of these operations have you done in your career so far?" he would probably say, "oh many," which would translate to perhaps ten or less. When one looks at Michael's nose you see a surgical tragedy caused by excessive surgery done at his insistence by doctors attempting to please a celebrity. It's sad to see this great talent labeled a "freak" by some.

Chapter One

The Early Days

IN SPUR, TEXAS Frank and Nancy Eliza Williams were blessed with a second set of twins. James Delbert and John Elbert born on March 8 and 9, 1921, (Jim was born before midnight and I was born after.) We chose to celebrate our birthdays on the 9th. We were the youngest of eight siblings, five girls and three boys. Father was a rancher turned house painter when he moved the family to the little town of Spur Texas. As you might know from it's name Spur was ranching and farming country. We had given up the ranch and moved into town. Our home was quite meager as evidenced by the fact that the kitchen had a dirt floor. We had a good-sized property because in those days land was cheap so we grew most of our food in well-tended sizeable gardens. Our mother was and excellent cook and even better at canning foods and storing them in the storm cellar.

Our neighbor to the south also had a major garden. They also raised pigs. I will never forget the ear piercing squeals of the pigs when the day came to kill and butcher one. We peaked through the fence and saw them cut the pig's throat. It was a haunting sight for young eyes to see. Then there was the day another neighbor's bull got lose and terrorized our neighborhood.

In keeping with the times we had no inside plumbing so there was the ever-present "outhouse." When Jim and I were around five or six years old we decided our outhouse needed painting. We found some old paint in the storm cellar. It was Kelly green. Our mother was busy and our father was away on a paint job so we had no supervision. We managed with the help of dad's ladder and paintbrushes to get the sides painted and left the top for last. It was a slanted surface and it was quite a struggle to get up there. We made it so we starting painting where we were at the low end and by the time we got to the upper end we were sitting in the paint. You can manage what our clothes looked like when we confessed to our mother what we had done.

There was a Mesa at the south end of town where people would go for Sunday picnics and to view the little town below. The most prominent structure in the vista below was our Kelly green outhouse.

One summer our mother decided we needed another chore. Our oldest sister, Frankie, was pregnant, not showing yet and our mother asked Jim and me if we would like to have a new little baby in the family. We said, "Yes but how do we get one?" She said, "If you save a hundred thread spools and send them off a stork will bring us a new baby." Over the next few months we knocked on the door of almost every home in Spur, Texas. It got to be a joke where people would say, "Don't answer the door it's those two little Williams boys asking for spools again." I'm not sure just how many spools we collected but Mom said it was enough and she took the cigar box full of spools and said she would mail them. When the day came and the stork was supposed to show up from the sky, we were sent to the neighbor's house across the street so "you won't scare the stork." We kept constant watch out the window and never saw a Stork. The new baby was, of course, a home delivery by ol' Dr. Nichols. Several years later while playing in the storm cellar we came across a cigar box full of spools.

The first doctor in our lives was this Dr. Nichols. He circumcised me when I was around six years old using open-drop ether anesthesia. It was the closest to being smothered to death that I could imagine.

I have a horrible memory of this experience to this day and a vowed that when I became a doctor I would never use this type of anesthesia on a patient.

THE WILLIAMS FAMILY SANTA MONICA, CALIFORNIA 1940

We had a family of eight siblings. There were two sets of twins, girls: Lucille and Lillian and ten years younger twin boys: James Delbert and John Elbert. Lolita, the oldest was a half sister. Next was Frankie and the youngest girl was Cora May (Moe).

MOTHER NANCY

The oldest male was William C. Williams, a brilliant, self-educated, engineer and inventor who led the family's migration to California. Lolita followed and became very successful in real estate as a broker in the Downy area near Los Angeles. The oldest full sister was Frankie and the youngest girl was Cora Mae nicknamed Moe after her married name Mohanna. Her husband volunteered to join the air force so he could fight the Japanese. They had shot down his younger brother. They got him too. Poor Moe was born between two sets of twins so you can imagine what her life was like. She had a congenital mouth deformity with large buckteeth that distorted her face. Moe had a beautiful body but her face was a terrible distraction. She was a fabulous dancer but none of her male classmates would ask her to dance. It was pathetic. During her senior year in Borger High School Dr. Waldo Beckley, a wonderful dentist friend did a radical resection of her entire upper jaw and made her a complete denture. I'll never forget when we first saw her. All of the tension had been released in her face and she was beautiful. She soon became the most popular girl in the school.

Mother had a double standard in the way she treated her daughters as compared to the boys. The girls had to be home no later than ten o'clock and she wanted to know what all they did for the whole evening. Her rules for us boys was, "I don't care what time you come in or what you do when you are out as long as you are good boys and never go to bed without coming into my room and kissing me good night."

THE BOYS AGES 3, 5 AND 13

This was great trust and we never disrespected the "good boys" part. In the light of today's theories on child rising she probably should have use the same psychology on the girls as she did us boys. It probably would have worked just as well with them.

In 1926 there was an oil boom in the Texas Panhandle. Father, Frank moved us there to a new little town later to be named Borger and joined the land rush along with some fifty thousand people all living in tents and make shift houses The town was corrupt requiring martial law by the Texas Rangers with their pearl handled guns and police dogs. A Barbed wire pen was constructed as a jail to throw the drunks in on Saturday night. This combined with oil well gushers coming in around the town was an exciting place for two wide-eyed kids to experience at

age five or six. The movie "Boom Town" with Clark Gable" was an ac-
curate story of this kind of an oil boomtown. The prosperity came to an
end with the great depression and stock market crash of 1929. Dad went
from a leaseholder to a house painter in order to get us through the hard
times. Mother, Nancy took in boarders after my dad put three little
houses together to create some extra sleeping rooms. Mother Nancy
was a strong lady who held the family together and managed to feed us
all when father, Frank was out of work or drunk.

DUST STORM IN TEXAS PANHANDLE

On Sunday April 14, 1935 a giant dust storm engulfed the Texas
Panhandle. Cyclic winds rolled up two miles high, stretched out a
hundred miles and moved faster than 50 miles an hour. These storms
destroyed vast areas of the Great Plains farmland. Every possible crack
was plugged, sheets were placed over windows and blankets were hung
behind doors. We held wet towels over our faces to filter as much of the
dust as possible. It was a very frightening experience but we survived.

JOHN AND JIM IN THEIR FIRST DRESS SUITS

Chapter Two

Borger High School

BORGER HIGH FOOTBALL TEAM

WE GRADUATED FROM Borger High School in 1939. Our home was on Coble St. and was turned into a boarding house shared with "rough-neck" oil field workers. Mother treated these men like they were her sons and they became a part of our family. Father, Frank, was an alcoholic, chain smoker who did painting and wallpaper hanging for a living. He developed emphysema, asthma and cirrhosis of the liver. Mother kicked him out of the house because of the drinking and abuse. She was intolerant and wouldn't allow even a beer in the house. He died of congestive heart failure.

No matter where we moved, one of the first things was to dig a storm cellar for refuge from the frequent tornadoes. It was also used for storage of canned foods and other survival items. After one tornado when we came up out of the cellar, we followed it's trail and saw some amazing things: a chicken running down the road cackling its head off, totally plucked, not a feather on it's body. There were straws driven through trees like tiny spears. A wagon had lost its wheels with the spokes piled up neatly beside the rims.

Jim and I got jobs at the Furr Food Store. Every Saturday for 16 hours work we were paid two dollars with two cents taken out for Social Security. We usually worked in the produce department, sacking ten-pound bags of potatoes and keeping the produce racks stocked and looking fresh. Our boss was a stern, grumpy man who always kept a bottle of whisky hidden in the large walk in freezer and especially on Saturday nights he would start nipping around six o'clock and by closing and clean up time at 11 o'clock he was pretty drunk. Our mother was very strict about drinking since our father did his share. We thought this was unacceptable behavior. One Saturday night we found his bottle in the cooler. It was about half empty by this time so we decided to add a little volume by pissing in it. Apparently he never knew the difference. We checked at the end of that night and the bottle was empty. We laughed but later felt guilty that we had done such a thing.

Frankie worked as a nurse for the most important role model in our lives. Dr. Walker, an elegant, well dressed, sterile looking man who always wore a fresh crisp white shirt and tie with a white handkerchief in his coat pocket. He was in great contrast to the other men that we met in this oil boom town, full of roughnecks and dirty looking people that are typically found in towns like Borger. We took our cuts and bruises to sister, Frankie, and Dr. Walker for repair and comfort. It was there that we decided we wanted to become doctors like this elegant man.

Chapter Three

College

OUR COLLEGE WAS Texas Technological in Lubbock, home of the Red Raiders football team. We waited tables in the boarding house for our room and board. The San Souci sorority had the most beautiful girls and we were always invited to their social functions. Ballroom dancing to tunes like "Tuxedo Junction" was the rage. My first college love was Mary Ann Stevenson a beautiful young lady who had her pick of the guys.

There was four of us pals from Borger, Texas who went to Texas Tech: Neal Nichols, Jay Barnett, brother, Jim and me. Nichols was by far the smartest and made straight A's with little effort.

Our Professor of English Literature was an interesting man. He had severe scoliosis, a twisted spine, often referred to as "hunch back." His deformity had a definite affect on his personality. He was brilliant, but down right nasty. He always rode a bicycle each day from his home to the school. His route passed a home where there was a large dog that barked at him every day. To protect himself he had a brick that he would pick up before reaching the house, carry it past the barking dog, put in a place so he could fine it and repeat the process in reverse on the way home. This went on for a full school year and then he found out the dog had a back injury and could not get off his porch.

The clock on the classroom wall was the kind that would run for a minute then jump to the next mark each time. We students found out that if we hit the clock with an eraser we could make the minute hand jump every time we hit it. Professor Strauss walked in one day and caught us throwing the erasers. He quietly picked up all the erasers and placed them on his desk. He then went to the blackboard where he wrote out an assignment for us to write an impromptu theme on any prediction that we might have for the future. He then sat in a chair with his humped back blocking the door. While we wrote, he threw erasers at the clock one by one until he had made it skip all the way to the end of the hour, at which time he called for the assignment.

The classroom was on the ground floor with large windows. He ordered us boys to open the windows, then turn our backs while the girls climbed out, then made us do the same. Usually we would have had a full hour to complete the assignment but with the help of the erasures he had cut our time down to about twenty minutes. Since I was a premed student, I chose the subject of surgery. I predicted that one day we would be able to stop the human heart, bypass it with some type of pump, repair it and then start it up again. I compared it to attempting to repair an auto engine while it was running. His usual custom was to grade an "F" if there was even one misspelled word. My spelling was correct but he gave me an "F" anyway and wrote in a heavy red marker across the top, "Preposterous, could never happen." Years later this cardiac surgery fantasy came true I remembered this and wished I had saved this essay so I could return it to Professor Strauss. I suspect that he was long gone by the time my prediction came true.

One Saturday afternoon the four of us were pondering the wonders of chemistry. We were on the subject of gases when someone mentioned that the human fart was composed of, among other things, methane gas. If so, one would assume that a fart would burn if lighted at the proper time. Barnett claimed to be the champion flautist in all of Texas. So he agreed to drop his pants, hoist his butt and when he was about to release his gas, Nichols was to have the lighted match ready. Jim was to stand by with a glass of water in order to douse any excess fire and I was to attempt to photograph the event with a small box camera. All went as planned. Barnett let go a whopper; Nichols applied the burning match at the precise time and a sizable, blue flame plumed up Barnett's back. As we were finishing this historic experiment, the door opened and in walked the priest who was making his rounds in the dorm to see if any of the students were in need of some spiritual guidance. There was Barnett with his bare ass exposed and all of us laughing at the size of the flame. When we explained, with embarrassment, what we were doing, the priest, in his Irish brogue said, "Glory be lads, could I see that for me self." So we repeated the experiment and we all enjoyed a hearty laugh.

We waited tables in the dorm, provided janitor service to the Engineering building at night, and did any type of odd jobs on campus. It wasn't easy but we managed.

Life at Texas Tech was special because it was a fairly small student body and the four of us were what you might call "big men on campus." We knew everyone and were always invited to the sorority functions and dances. We were happy and our grades were all A's and B's which were plenty good enough to qualify for medical school.

UCLA / USC

At the end of our sophomore year (1941) we transferred to UCLA in California with the help of brother, Bill. By that time he had become an important tooling engineer at Douglas Aircraft in Santa Monica. He got us jobs on the swing shift so we could work to support ourselves and continue school at the same time. A full schedule with school in the mornings and swing shift jobs at Douglas (circa 1941). Living with brother, Bill and his wife Virginia. UCLA was a huge change. Not only were the classes large, sometimes consisting of a hundred or more students but they were much more difficult with a whole different style of teaching. The social life was aloof and hard to penetrate. Unless we were members of one of the fraternities we felt insignificant. This, plus our schedule of working the swing shift at Douglas Aircraft Company gave us very little extra time to study much less to join in the social life off campus. Having a car was a necessity so thanks to the job on the swing shift at Douglas we were able to buy our first car.

OUR FIRST CAR. A FORD

With such a heavy schedule we became depressed and our grades suffered. We were two poor little Texas boys completely out of our element. By this time Jim and I realized that the UCLA transfer was really a bad idea and we had bitten off more than we could chew, trying to work and attend a difficult school at the same time. We decided that we had to return to Texas Tech to finish our pre med requirements or we would have little chance of being accepted to any good medical school. After a year back at Texas Tech we became brave enough to attempt California once again and elected to enroll in USC so we might have a better chance to be accepted to their medical school. Having learned the value of being in a fraternity at UCLA we pledged the SAE house and were accepted into the world of the fraternity life. This gave us a feeling of belonging, our insecurity was nourished and we did much better.

One Sunday while washing our car, the news of the Pearl Harbor bombing came over the radio. Jim and I were feeling so patriotic that even though we were accepted to medical school we decided to join the Naval Air Force and go to Med. School later. In the process of joining up we had an interview with a Naval Commander who did us the greatest service. He said, "Boys, since I see that you have already been accepted to Medical School, I think you should go ahead with that because in time we may need you far more as doctors than as pilots. We have plenty of volunteers for pilots." We took his advice and went on to Medical School.

Chapter Four

Medical School

THE YEARS SPENT at the University of Maryland Medical School in Baltimore were 1943 to 1947. Brother, Jim was elected president of our freshman class and I was called "the power behind the throne." Life in the fraternity house was fascinating. Each freshman was assigned an upper classman adviser. My adviser took us to the burlesque show in a bad part of Baltimore on our first evening, which was some beginning. I suppose he figured there would be plenty of time for the more serious stuff that was to come. It turned out to be the routine: work hard all week then play hard on the weekends and the burlesque happened to be on Saturday night.

One day we had a discussion with Jose Valdares, the youngest member of our class (22-year-old) about which specialty we might like to pursue. Pediatrics: who wants to deal with screaming kids all day? Obstetrics: who wants to be getting up every night to deliver babies when we know most of them are born at night because most of them are conceived at night? Dermatology: who wants to deal with ugly skin rashes? Orthopedics: dealing with backaches all the time is a pain in the neck. Surgery: all that blood and guts, yuck! Internal medicine: heart attacks, sick and dying people with cancers and bizarre diseases. Psychiatry: maybe? Gnaw; these people rarely get well and besides who wants to deal all day with crazy people. Neurosurgery: who could deal with brain tumors that are rarely curable? No way! After this conversation, Jose said, "we've eliminated everything so what the hell are we doing here in med school?" Never the less we stayed and became doctors. Jose, handsome Latino from Puerto Rico, became a gynecologist because he loved women so much.

We have all been led to believe that we should respect our teachers. The epitome of a teacher and the source of unquestioned authority is the "professor." I'm not sure about other fields of endeavor but in the profession of Plastic Surgery, the professor image has, in my experience, not lived up to the expectations. In fact some of the most weird and even bazaar people I have know have occupied the chair as head of surgical department in some of our major universities. It has been said that a good number of full time university teaches take those jobs simply because they could not make a living in the outside competitive world of a private practice. This is not true in some instances when the doctor truly enjoys teaching and in particular research with its intellectual reward.

The professor of anatomy was our first in medical school. He was an old German by the name of Uhlenhouth. A lion of a man with an unruly mane of gray hair. He was a real taskmaster and would tolerate no nonsense. He would have made a good Nazi. Then there was Dr. Figgie, a roly poly, assistant professor who had married Uhlenhouth's daughter.

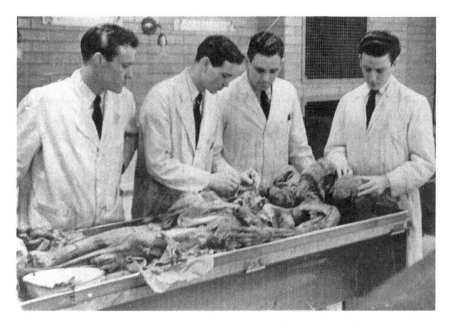

ANATOMY LAB

Doctor Uhlenhouth's Anatomy class was setup in the basement of the medical school with special tables for the cadavers (dead people). We were assigned four students per table (see photo) and our cadaver was a male. We gave him the name of "Toby" and grew to respect and thank him for contributing his dead body so we could learn.

We first skinned his extremities in order to uncover every nerve, vein, muscle, tendon and bone, understanding all the relationships and the magnificent design of the Human body.

Those early days in the anatomy lab made it difficult to sleep at night knowing that we had spent a good part of the day dissecting a real human and the wonderment of what kind of a life this man might have had. After a few months we became so blasé about working on ol' Toby that we could spread out our lunch on his chest and eat while dissecting him without one hint of nausea.

There were only four female students in our class and they happened to be assigned to a male cadaver. When it came time for them to dissect his reproductive organs all of us male students stood around their table to watch them. I must say the ladies handled it very well.

Neuroanatomy was a separate department and the lectures were given by a heavy set doctor who was always in a hurry and was constantly heard to say, "we have so much to do and so little time to do it in." He had spent several years researching the number of Betts cells in the human brain. Then he found out that someone had done it all several years earlier. He never made up for the lost time. The gynecology professor lectured one day on the muscular component of the female vagina and he related a story of a stripper he once knew who could actually smoke a cigar with her vagina. A week or so later some of the students rigged a small pulley from the ceiling over the lectern and in the midst of his lecture they lowered a cigar until it dangled just in front of him.

Brother Jim was such an eager student that he was always the first to volunteer for anything new. Our first day in gynecology clinic the instructor asked us who would like to be the first to do a pelvic examination. Of course Jim's hand went up before anyone else. The nurse had placed the patient on the pelvic table with her legs in the stirrups. She was behind a curtain and draped so it was difficult to see at first that she was quite obese. The procedure is for the examiner to sit on a stool between the patient's legs, take the vaginal speculum in the dominant hand, spread the labia with the other hand and insert the speculum. Jim did everything properly. He spread the fat legs first with hands, then his elbows, then moved his hand higher then his elbows again but could not find the vagina. He literally disappeared in the patient's obesity. The patient had agreed to this procedure to help the instructor teach the medical students that there were some patients on which it was impossible to do a routine pelvic exam. It was quite funny and it cured Dr. Jim from ever volunteering to be first again.

Dr. Jim married Henrietta, the Neurosurgical scrub-nurse at University Hospital. Mother, Nancy Eliza, came to Baltimore for the wedding and again for our graduation. Father, Frank had died during our second year in Medical School.

We had been on an accelerated schedule in Medical School due to the war so we were given nine months off in order to get back on the September to June schedule. Brother Jim and I decided to do an externship at Santa Monica Hospital. This was like an Internship before graduation and we learned a lot and met some interesting people. I remember their admitting a little girl around age seven for acute tonsillitis. She wasn't famous at that time put her father was. He was Henry Fonda and this was his daughter, Jane.

MARRIAGE NUMBER ONE

JEANNE—THE FIRST WIFE AND A 1ODAY MARRIAGE

It was during this period of Externship that I meet the lady that was to become my first wife. Her name was Donna Jeanne Honrath, a native of Las Vegas, Nevada. Her father was a wealthy developer. When she was a child of ten or eleven she came home one day after school, went to the garage to feed her pet rabbit and found her mother hanging from a rafter, a suicide. One can imagine the affect it had on her for the rest of her life. In an attempt to offset the tragic experience, her father showered her with anything she wanted no matter what it

21

was. This over indulgence played a major role in her life and made her almost impossible to please.

Jeanie had come to the hospital to visit her girl friend that had been in an accident and was recovering from a broken leg. This friend who was soon to leave the hospital told me that seeing me several times Jeanie said, "I'm going to marry that young doctor no matter what it takes." Since this young lady was used to getting anything she wanted, little did I know that I was in for trouble.

Jim and I lived at the hospital during the externship. Our room was in the southwest wing in a semi basement with easy access to the back entrance of the hospital. Late one evening while enjoying a night off duty in our little room alone their came a soft knock on the door. There she was. "May I come in? I just stopped buy to thank you for taking such good care of my friend." she said. What she didn't say was that now she was there to "take care of me."

A few weeks later I was given the news that would test my integrity and future forever. She was pregnant. Now came the integrity part. Should I marry the lady or seek an abortion? In those days abortion was highly illegal and besides it seemed an ugly choice. My mother had always taught us that if you ever get a girl in trouble you should honor her by making an honest woman of her. Since I was due back in Baltimore in September, we had a quickie marriage in Las Vegas. Jeanie was Catholic so the ceremony was performed in the Church. Her father gave her another new car and placed in her name only. We left for the long drive to Baltimore. It took a full ten days to make the trip. During the entire trip I was unable to select a restaurant, hotel, motel, or anything else that pleased my new wife. She found fault with every thing I did including the driving of her new car. The final insult came when we arrived back in Baltimore and she got a look at the tiny apartment I had reserved for us. Because of the war economy, good, inexpensive apartments were hard to find. The kitchen was so small that it accommodated only one person at a time. There was a fairly good size living room that was also the bedroom. The building was in a good part of town on Euclid Avenue and I felt that we were very lucky to have the place.

After a brief walk through she said, "I can't live here, this is awful!" I responded with, "Were would you like to live?" "At the Lord Baltimore Hotel. My dad will pay for it." This happened to be the most expensive hotel in the city. I knew that I had made a terrible mistake. Even though I had done the honorable thing and my conscious was clear, I knew that if I kept this lady with me I would do one of two things, I would either flunk out of med school or I would have to kill her. I chose the legal way so I said, "Jeannie, I think you should get in that new car of yours, that we haven't even unpacked yet, and go back to your daddy in Las Vegas. I can not afford you." That's exactly what she did. Later, she gave birth to my first son, John Christopher.

Chris was a beautiful boy. I saw very little of him during the first year of his life. By this time I was doing the internship at the Good Samaritan Hospital in Los Angeles and Chris was with his mother in Las Vegas, Nevada. Sometime during his first year of his life he became ill with meningitis. This left him with some damage to his brain resulting

in occasional seizures. On September 26, 2000 he underwent Brain Surgery for his seizures. His postoperative period was complicated by depression and paranoia that lasted two to three years. It takes a long time for the brain to recover from injury or surgery. He is much better now. During this period he needed support and understanding from his wife and daughter. Instead they abandoned him. He is a fine young man with College degrees. He was married one time to Joyce and had a daughter, Christina who is my first grand daughter. Chris has owned his own machine tool company and is now a Real Estate agent. He is living with me and has helped me tremendously with this book.

NAVY

In 1945, during world war two, there was a need for doctors so those of us who were already in medical school were allowed to finish in one of the government-sponsored programs.

It was the V-12 program sponsored by the US. Navy that helped Jim and me through the first two and one half years of Medical School. As students of the Navy we were given the status of "Mid Shipman" and were required to wear the uniforms. This was the equivalent to being enrolled at the Naval Academy in Annapolis, Maryland. What a good deal! It helped us, old Texas boys, to become doctors. Our agreement with the Navy was that we would serve two years on active duty as medical officers. This came in the nick of time because we were running out of money and would not have been able to finish. Student loans were not available at that time. We were so happy with the deal that we would have volunteered to give back even more time if the Navy needed us. A generous brother-in-law, Ollie Hare, had sponsored us for the last year. Without him and the Navy we would have never made it.

SCHOOL AS MIDSHIPMAN US NAVY

Without Jeanne, we managed to complete the last year of medical school. By this time Dr. Jim had married Henrietta, a nurse who worked at the University Hospital in the neurosurgical department. She was a beautiful young "Florence Nightingale" who had inherited a very unusual breast overgrowth to an enormous degree. This of course required radical surgical reduction. At that time the sophistication in reconstructing surgery was not as it is today. The result was quite deforming, complicated by severe postoperative infection and at that time there were no Silicone implants or good antibiotics to help with the problem. She went for many years with terrible scars and no breast at all. I marveled at the way brother, Jim handled his wife's deformity. He did not allow this to affect their marital relationship at all. They went on to have five children. I was very proud of him.

Chapter Five

Internship

WE CHOSE TO do our internship at The Hospital of the Good Samaritan in Los Angeles. We were furnished room and board. The house staff quarters were excellent but our duties gave us very little time to spend there. We were paid a handsome $100 a month. There wasn't much time for a social life but there were some very attractive young ladies in the Nursing School. During our year as interns some famous people were admitted, the most interesting was Howard Hughes after his famous airplane crash.

During the break between out junior and senior years and after our externship at the Santa Monica Hospital the Navy assigned us to duty as lab technicians at the U.S. Naval Air Station, Corpus Christy, Texas. One of my unpleasant duties was to oversee the morgue. Since this was a training facility for beginning pilots, crash accidents were not uncommon. One evening I was called to open the morgue to receive the bodies of an instructor and his student pilot, killed when their plane crashed on takeoff. It was quite painful to see such a loss of two fine young men. In sorting through their personal effects I learned that the student pilot was from California. In his wallet there was a photo of a beautiful young lady that was his wife. They had been married for just a short time. Two years later I met this lady under unusual circumstances. After graduating from Med. School, we were doing the internship at the Good Samaritan Hospital in Los Angeles. One of our best general surgeons, Dr. Nichols was admitted to my floor to have his gall bladder removed the next morning. I went to his room to do the routine history and physical exams. Dr. Nichols was in his robe, sitting in a bedside chair. His daughter was lounging on his bed with her hands folded behind her head. When she looked up and saw me she made a gasping sound as though she had seen a ghost, and started to cry. I had never experienced that kind of reaction from anyone before. I apologized and started to leave the room. She said, "Oh no! Please don't go. I'm sorry. You reminded me so much of my husband it was a shock to me when I first saw your face." As she wiped her tears with the back of her hand she told me that her young husband was a Navy Pilot and had been killed in a plane crash in Corpus Christy, Texas. I recognized her from the photo I had seen in his wallet. It was her husband that I had put into the morgue that sad evening in Corpus Christy. There is no way I could ever tell her about this bizarre coincident.

Dr. Nichols had his gall bladder surgery without complications and was back in the O.R. at Good Sam in a few weeks. As I was scrubbed on one of his cases, I asked about his daughter. He said, "She hasn't gotten over meeting you yet and wanted me to invite you to dinner at our home." I was delighted because I found her very appealing and I was a great admirer of her father. The dinner was elegant and I got to meet her mother and feel the warmth of their home. We dated several times after that evening and all she talked about was her dead husband and compared me to him in every way. I was feeling quite serious about her but became convinced that I could never replace her husband. In her memory he was perfect and I would always be just a substitute for her tragic loss. It was painful for both of us but I stopped seeing her.

Chapter Six

Residency at Kern General Hospital

AT THAT TIME, 1947, we were required to complete one full year of rotating internship and to take and pass the California State Medical Board Examination before we were allowed to start practice as doctors. Our one-year internship had only served to whet our appetite for more training, as we still wanted to be Surgeons.

We heard of a hospital in Bakersfield, California the Kern County General Hospital that offered a pretty good package. As first year rotating surgical residents we were given a cottage and a monthly stipend of $150.00. We could pick up another $35.00 by working the emergency room on a rotating basis from five P.M. until eight A.M. the next day. The only problem here was that we could count on one or two hours of sleep if we were lucky. We were expected to go directly to our respective floors the next day to be available for our regular duties.

The hospital had an arrangement worked out with the state of California to cover the state women's prison in Tehachapi. This was a much sought after deal because the pay was about $150.00 for our services. We rotated on this assignment among the staff and one of us would go up to Tehachapi for six to eight hours, one or two days a month to run their clinic, for the inmates. These doctor visits were among the few close encounters these inmates could have with men.

28

The appointment list was long and most of the complaints required a pelvic exam.

The Emergency Room at Kern General was extremely busy. The highway yielded a constant stream of trauma cases, the well-known endemic of San Jauquine Valley year, and of all things an epidemic of Polio.

Dr. Jim's story: *"Kern County Hospital was terribly under staffed at that time and after I had been there for about four months, even though I was supposed to be in a rotating surgical residency, it became my turn to cover the infectious disease ward of the hospital. I was placed in charge of the ward and reported for duty. When I first went out on the floor to see what we had in the way of patients, I heard a loud noise that was rhythmical but with a strong moaning quality. I investigated the source of the noise and was surprised to find that it was emitted by the bellows of a crude iron lung. This was called a Heidabrink iron lung. It had to be one of the oldest and the worst designs I can ever remember seeing. This thing looked like it was made in someone's garage. It was somewhat rectangular and was made from pieces of cold rolled steel that had been welded together. It had two portholes on each side for the nurses to work through and one larger one, at one end for the patient's head. I cannot remember how one would get the head through the larger opening - probably like a guillotine but it was secure enough to allow the bellows to assist the patient's breathing. The action of the bellows creates a negative pressure inside of the iron lung and the chest muscles, being weak or paralyzed, allow the chest to expand. When the chest expands air is drawn in through the patient's mouth or nose, into the lungs thereby supplying the patient's need for oxygen. The chest muscles and their elasticity is then released by the momentary pause of the bellows, thereby allowing the patient to exhale. This is again repeated over and over again and is surprisingly effective in meeting the patient's oxygen needs.*

There was a young lady in this noisy device that had been there for

*several days. She had acute bulbar poliomyelitis and was totally depen-
dent on the iron lung to keep her alive. She had another reason to stay
alive - she was about eight months pregnant. The nurses loved her, as she
was indeed a very special person. She never complained and the nursing
staff would each day brush her long blond hair that was draped over
the small headrest. Little did I know at that time that we were on the
very beginning of a severe epidemic of poliomyelitis? Susan was one of, if
not the first case to be admitted. This was long before Dr. Jonas Salk's
polio vaccination was developed. All we had to treat the patient with at
that time were the Kinney hot packs, which consisted of a piece of pure
wool that was heated in a steaming hot vat. The heat helped relieve some
of the muscle cramps that were so prevalent in this condition. The hot
packs were placed directly on the painful area. We are indebted to sister
Kinney, a registered nurse, who observed that for some reason, if the hot
pack was cotton or even partially cotton it would result in a severe burn
and blistering of the patient.*

*The epidemic moved in with all of its fury. We admitted on the aver-
age of eleven new patients each day. Many of them had bulbar polio so we
needed more iron lungs. We would rotate the patients in the iron lungs
so as to help as many as possible. Some of them needed only intermittent
help. Even though I had a wife and two young children the thought only
fleetingly crossed my mind that I was putting them at risk by taking care
of the polio patients. There was just too much to do without worrying
about something that I could do nothing about.*

*Each day I would spend a lot of time with Susan, the patient that was
pregnant and had been moved into a new and better iron lung. She continued to get weaker in spite of the efforts of the nursing staff by this time
I knew her and her husband and family very well. It was obvious that she
was not going to live long. I talked with her husband and told him that
I had a plan that had a chance of, at best, to save the life of their baby.
My plan was to do an immediate caesarean section if the mother did
indeed die. I received the permission of her husband after our discussion*

and began immediately to implement the plan. We made up a special sterile surgical pack and placed it just outside of her room. We were ready to go with the plan. The admitting of the patients with polio continued unabated. I hated to leave town as it came to be my turn to go up to the women's state prison but I really needed the extra money. I went up early in the morning to Tehachapi and spent the whole day running the clinic. It was quite late in the evening when I got home and I had an urgent telephone call waiting. In those days we had no portable telephones or car phones. (This was back in late October of 1948)

The call was from the nurse in charge of the polio ward. Knowing of my continued interest in the patient she had called to tell me that Susan was in labor and could I come right over. It did not matter that I was not on call for the ward that evening. I wanted to be there for her delivery. When I arrived I did find her in full labor and my examination revealed that the cervix or opening of the womb was almost completely dilated. We were very concerned that the baby was in distress as we could not hear or find a fetal heart beat. We started giving her oxygen by mask in an attempt to get some to the baby.

The evening wore on, as did her labor. The delivery was imminent after a few hours and I got ready, as did one of the nurses. We worked through the portholes in the side of the iron lung. It was not long until she started her delivery and it was only at that time that it became obvious that she was having a breach delivery. I had attended several deliveries in the past but this would be my first breach delivery. Wouldn't you know that it would have to be in an iron lung?   *

The baby was "still born" and had been dead for some time. The mother was still awake and it was my job to tell her that the baby was not living. She was of course devastated to say the least and finally closed her eyes and never opened them again. She lived just long enough to deliver the baby - and then she died.   *.

I felt terrible and responsible in some way for all of this. It was my first death in my young career as a doctor.

I don't really know how I found my way back to our cottage as my eyes were filled with tears. I cried like a baby until finally, exhausted, I fell asleep.

The next morning I dreaded going back to the hospital. When I walked into the ward there, in that same iron lung, was another victim similar in age and looks to Susan - she, however, was not pregnant.

Finally there were signs of the epidemic letting up. We were admitting fewer patients and we began a deep and prolonged sigh of relief. When I first arrived on this infectious disease service we had the one and only iron lung, the one that made all of the noise. When I left the floor we had thirteen new iron lungs and were rotating the patients through these in order to meet the demand. Believe me, years later when Dr. Salk came up with the polio-vaccine, my wife, our five children and I all were among the very first in town to have the vaccine. I had seen far too much polio in the past and hoped and prayed that I would never see any more.

I continued my rotating surgical residency until March of 1949 and had kept in touch with my government obligations. I knew that I was going to have to go back into the Navy again to give the government some time to compensate for their paying for the first two and one half years of my four years of medical school. It did not matter to me that there was talk around that the government was about to draft some, if not all of the young doctors that had been sent to medical school. To my knowledge it was the only draft that was ever 'instigated' for one class of citizens. Our choice was one of two options, one, we could go into the service as a Lieutenant junior grade or secondly, stand a very good chance of being drafted with the rank of private 1st. Class. There is, of course, considerable difference. I did not mind at all serving my time for without the Navy-V12 program we would never have been able to graduate from medical school."

Chapter Seven

The Professors

PROFESSOR FURNACE

This professor and head of the Plastic Surgery Division in Irvine, California has an obsession with timepieces. He may be found on a certain day wearing two or more watches on each arm and one or two on each ankle, and there would be two or more of the stick on type clocks on the dashboard of his car. Each watch had an alarm set for different times for certain appointments of the day. On one afternoon while traveling to some University clinics with his residents he interrupted the conversation by asking, "Does any one know what time it is?"

PROFESSOR SHAW

Dr. William Shaw was appointed to head the department of Plastic and Reconstructive Surgery at UCLA after a search to bring in some expert from afar because we all know they are always better than the people we have on staff already. However, this new person must have some exotic or highly specialized talent to bring to the job. Dr. Shaw was born in China but grew up in this country. He was trained in New York with an emphasis on micro vascular surgery. This specialty requires the use of the surgical microscope and a steady control of very tiny instruments. The suture material is so fine it is hard to see with the naked eye. I have always admired physicians that go into that field because they are able to move large amounts of tissue to where ever it is needed by putting together very small blood vessels sometimes smaller than one to two millimeters in diameter. This creates instant blood supply so the flaps will survive. It is not always successful but in a large percentage of cases it works very well and is a tremendous advance in reconstructive surgery. The recent patient in Paris, France who had a partial face transplant done is a good example of this microsurgical technique. Now the problem with Professor Shaw is that this procedure is what he likes to do and would prefer moving a large hunk of buttock tissue up to enlarge the breasts rather than using a simple silicone breast implant. Shaw's procedure leaves scarring and contour deformity of the buttock. To justify his procedure Dr. Shaw bought into the "fiction" that Silicone gel breast implants are toxic and cause connective tissue disease. After years of clinical studied and research there has been no evidence that Silicone gel causes any of the diseases the lawyers claim it does.

PROFESSOR RALPH MILLARD

Dr. Ralph Millard, professor and chairman of the Plastic and Reconstructive Surgery Department at the University of Miami School of medicine. He is a brilliant and superbly talented surgeon who coauthored a set of books with Sir Harold Gilles who is considered by some to be one of the fathers of modern plastic surgery. After reading these highly illustrated books, I was instantly converted from the agonizing business of general surgery with it's sickness, cancer, and deaths, to the creative, positive and happy specialty of plastic and reconstructive surgery. These were fascinating books full of gore pictures of severe injuries resulting from the tragedies of both world war one and two. But even with such a macabre subject there were illustrations of incredibly creative and ingenious techniques of reconstructing faces and other body parts torn away by the insanity of war. These books were, in a sense the history of plastic surgery. They illustrated how the trench warfare injuries created the need and met the challenge to develop techniques and procedures that had never been done before. Many of these facial injuries requiring "tubed pedicle" flaps. These consisted of a segment of abdominal skin, lifted, sutured into a tube and left attached at one end and the other end attached to the arm. When the blood supply had developed from the arm the abdominal end would be detached, and then rotated up to the face. After another three to six weeks the tube would survive from it's new blood supply from the face and it would then be ready to be used to replace the lost tissue for rebuilding facial structures. Most of these patients were kept in a special hospital near London, called Rocksdown House and they referred to themselves as the "Guinea Pig Club."

Dr. Millard is a no nonsense type of fellow and definitely does not like to waste his time on students and even his patients unless there is good reason. His many contributions to the literature include a beautiful technique on the repair of cleft lip in children; sometimes referred to a "hare lip" deformity and he mastered the technique to perfection. The photographs of his results that were seen in his published papers were so good that it was sometimes rumored that he surely must have had the photos retouched because it was thought that no one could possibly make those children look so normal as he had. During the early days of my training I attended the famous symposium of Baker and Gordon in Miami, Florida, which is held every year and always features some well-known expert from afar and occasionally some of the local guys. On the program that year was "Cleft Lip Repair". Well here in Miami lived one of the world recognized experts and authorities on this procedure, Dr. Ralph Millard. Drs. Baker and Gordon, who were well known in their own right were not fond of Dr. Millard because he was felt to be arrogant and condescending with no time or courtesy to the average human being and specially his competitors who were definitely not on his level. Millard was not invited to be on the program. Three of us from California who were quit enamored with Dr. Millard's work felt somewhat cheated so we, naively, thought of calling his home on a Saturday to ask if we might come by and spend a few minutes with him that afternoon after the finish of the symposium. At the time, I was still in training with Dr. Albert Davis in San Francisco, who had himself spent time in his early years training with Sir Harold Gilles. Dr. E.C. Brown, who was in practice with Davis, we felt was the best choice to make the call. The third member of our little group was Dr. Matthew Gleason from San Diego, a very humorous fellow.

Brown made the phone call but no one answered the phone; it was definitely off the hook. It seemed that other people from the symposium had the same idea that we had. We decided since this was our last day in Miami that we would chance it to just go to his house and ring his door bell. We asked E.C. Brown to approach his front door while Matt and I hid in the car. Millard answered the door in his Bermuda shorts, obviously enjoying his weekend. After what looked like a serious conversation, Brown came back to the car and said. "He's not very happy that we have intruded on his privacy but if we were really serious about learning he would be willing to give us only fifteen or twenty minutes because he was busy writing a book." We ran to his house and were ushered in to his study. We sat humbly at his feet while he quizzed us to see if we knew enough about his work to justify his discussing it with us. He turned to me and said, "Do you understand what "C" flap is in the operation?" I said, "yes, sir. That's the little flap that is based on the columella which when rotated laterally creates the sill of the nasal floor." He replied that I had passed the test and he could talk to me and since the other guys were there they could listen.

This was a most interesting and rewarding conversation and as he warmed to the respect we showed him he even served us tea. Two hours later he said the visit was over but if we were really serious he would send us to the Jackson Memorial Hospital where he just happened to have five children that he had operated on a few days previously. He said, "Now I won't call to tell the nurses to let you in the ward unless you are sure that you will go." We replied in unison, "Yes, sir, Yes sir, we'll go there right now."

We arrived at the hospital and as we went from crib to crib examining those children, none of the three of us said a word. We just looked with amazement at how beautiful each little mouth appeared with perfect cupids bows and symmetry. We left the ward and walked quietly to the elevator, not saying a word. As we punched the elevator button to go down, Matt Gleason broke the silence when he said, "Do you think he retouched those kids?"

HAROLD SILVER

Harold and Lynda Silver live in Toronto, Canada. He has a very good practice in the famous old Royal York hotel. Following surgery he keeps all his patients overnight in the hotel. The next morning he has them take their bandages off shower and gently wash and blow-dry their hair. He has the women put on light makeup, and then come down to the office. They feel fresh, clean and look good. He has them take a walk, weather permitting to stimulate their total blood supply to the surgical areas. It's amazing how happy they are with their new look and their physical well being.

Harold is a great friend and an excellent surgeon. He has a wonderful sense of humor and enjoys poking fun at us Americans. He says, "You Americans talk too much. You give the patient an hour lecture on the technique, benefits and possible complications of surgery. The patients don't want to hear all of that. They want to know only two things: What can you do and how much."

I met Harold and Lynda in Miami at one of the early Baker and Gordon Seminars. At the time Lynda was working for Howard Gordon. Harold took her away and married her. They have made a fine marriage and have one son. Harold got, not only a fine wife but also a super scrub nurse assistant. They make a very good team. We speak on the phone frequently and enjoy sharing our experiences and currant thinking. There's always a good new joke or two from Harold and I really look forward to these calls. He says he likes to talk to me because he thinks I'm honest with no BS. I hope so.

HAROLD SILVER AND ME

A long time friend of Harold Silvers was a London Plastic Surgeon, Philip LeBon. He had a quaint office that was dominated by a big dog that always lay in the center passage. Everyone including the patients had to step over him to get to the exam rooms. He was outrageous to say the least. On one of his trips to London, Harold paid a visit to Phillip's home. It was in the evening at cocktail hour.

He found his host in the garden, sitting with a drink in one hand and a leash in the other. The other end of the leash was around the neck of a nude lady.

I met Phillip at the Baker and Gordon Seminar in Miami. The cocktail conversation at these meeting was always dominated by "Shop Talk" At a lull in the conversation Phillip LeBon asked an interesting question, "Do you get good results with your surgery?" We all said, "Yes." His reply was, "I don't." "Then why do you do the surgery?" He was asked. "I don't know anything else to do."

IVO PITANGUY

When the Shah of Iran was alive and in power his entire royal family was enamored with plastic surgery. In particular they liked American surgeons. However, one of the firsts summoned to work on the Queen was Ivo Pitanguy of Rio de Janeiro. The Queen was to have breast implants. For the sake of privacy the

PITANGUY AND ME WHEN WE WERE INDUCTED AS FELLOWS IN THE AMERICAN COLLAGE OF SURGEONS.

Shah wanted Ivo to do the surgery in the palace where a special OR was to be set up. After careful consideration Pitanguy wisely opted to use the local hospital, so a whole floor was isolated for the Queen. Immediately following the operation the patient bled requiring blood transfusions that would not have been available in the Palace. In spite of this frightful episode Ivo made a good impression on the royal family. A year or so later he came to San Francisco to be inducted into the American College of Surgeons at the same time I was. He came without his wife, Marilou. I was with my then wife Shannon/Mary whom Ivo knew very well because he had been a guest in our home and we had made a visit to his in Rio. We were having dinner with him at Ondines Restaurant in Sausilito at which time he related to us the detail story of his service to the queen. When he had finished I asked him the sixty four dollar question, "What did you charge the Shah for you service? His reply was, "how does one set a fee for a king? You pack up your things, say good bye, go home and wait for the presents to arrive". During the whole story he had his shoe off and was playing with Shannon's leg under the table. I was so fascinated with his story that I had not noticed my wife's squirming.

When Ivo visited our home in Beverly Hills, Shannon did every thing she could to entertain him, arranged a tennis game, called on one of her attractive girl friends to accompany him for lunch at the Bistro Garden, took him shopping etc. When the day was over and before I came home from the office, Ivo had showered and was standing at the top of the stairs in his robe and clogs looking sorrowful. Shannon noticed and asked him what was the matter. He said, "I have had a wonderful day but you have not tamed the lion in me."

Ivo Pitanguy, the man from lpanema, Brazil's most famous professor, a handsome, dark, well built but short in stature with a strong eye for the ladies, especially blond ladies. lvo made his international reputation on his publications and PR espousing body sculpturing and breast reductions. In Brazil the women seem to be more plump and busty, so for every woman in the USA who has her breasts enlarged there is one in Brazil who has them reduced.

My acquaintance with Ivo began in 1974 when the Aesthetic Society was small enough that we could have our meeting aboard a cruise ship in the Caribbean. The SS Southward was the name of the ship and it was completely booked by plastic surgeon from around the world. The intimate and confined space of a ship allowed everyone aboard to get to know each other quite well. It was on this Plastic Surgery Cruise that I encouraged Dr. Jack Sheen, the renowned (in my opinion the worlds best nasal surgeon) when he gave his first presentation to his peers. By the time we had finished giving our papers and the ship had returned to port in Miami, I had an invitation to visit Dr. Pitanguy in Rio. More correctly, Mary, my wife at the time, who was young, blond, and beautiful, was invited to Rio and I of course was expected to come along if I wanted to. Ivo loves blondes. No matter why I was invited, it was a great opportunity to learn and have a great experience. The Pitanguy's lived in a beautiful estate in the suburbs of Rio located on what looked like about five acres. A tall fence protected the property from the outside world and to secure the home even more, the care taker allowed six of the most ferocious dogs one could imagine, to roam the grounds at night. He called them "Doggies." These were huge animals with heads as large as those of a lion. Ivo said that if anyone came into the grounds the dogs would kill them. One evening after dinner my host wanted to play a set of tennis, The court was about fifty yards from the main house and the dogs had been let loose. I mentioned the fact to Ivo and he casually stated that as long as I was with him the dogs wouldn't bother me. I said, "Ivo, the only way you can get me to the tennis court with those monsters out would be to carry me." We played tennis another day.

The Pitanguy Clinic consisted of a small specialty hospital with twenty-six beds all private rooms. The surgical suite had three operating rooms superbly equipped with a first rate staff. There were three teams of surgeons. The routine was for the professor, Dr. Pitanguy, to start the operation, do the basic incisions and dissection, set the key sutures then one of the teams would come in, remove the key sutures stop the bleeding and finish the operation. The chief would spend no more than thirty minutes on each case while the full length of the procedure would be three to four hours. This way the volume of surgery done and the income was easily tripled or quadrupled.

When the morning surgery schedule was finished Ivo would retreat to his special office in the penthouse atop the hospital for lunch and a message. His route from the surgery suite to the penthouse was through an attack type passage in order to avoid the post operative patients, many of whom would be waiting at their doorway to see him if he used the normal hall way.

While his German masseur gave him his message his secretary would read him the daily mail and he would dictate the answers. His day's schedule was carefully designed to allow the maximum use of his time. We did have some time to discuss the techniques and surgical philosophies he taught. For instance his fondness for body sculpting, which accounted for a good bit of his notoriety, was no longer his favorite procedures. He finally admitted, what many of us in America had concluded that the scars created by these operations were excessive and amounted to "trading one defect for another" and this we considered not to be a good trade. He admitted that he was at that time doing less and less of these procedures. This was long before the era of liposuction. His breast reductions and face-lifts were very good. Among other subjects we discussed the handling of patients and their demand for perfection. He summed this part up by saying, "Plastic surgery would be fun if it weren't for the patients"

Pitanguy owned a private island off the coast, about a half-hour small plane ride from Rio. The landing strip was not lighted so the trip had to be made during day light hours. A trip to the island was on the agenda for one-week end while we were there. The schedule was for us to leave the small airport near the harbor around four o'clock Friday afternoon. I had mentioned to Ivo that I wanted to buy some special surgical instruments while there. He failed to tell me that we needed to leave before dark. By the time I found the proper address we had wondered through the bowels of Rio and through some of it's worst areas. After becoming lost several times we arrived to learn that

Dr. Pitanguy had called to ask that the instruments be made while I waited. After returning to Ivo's home it was after five o'clock. I learned that my wife, Mary had already left with Ivo and Celsius, his twelve-year-old son. In order to make the flight before dark I was to take a taxi. Flavio, the home decorator happened to be there and gave this information to me. Mrs. Pitanguy was at a school function for one of her other children and was to come to the island the following morning. The decorator, a young man about thirty years of age, offered to take me on his motorcycle because he thought we could possibly make it quicker that way. Before I had time to think rationally, I was on the back of this monster machine going hell bent through rush hour traffic at the worst time of the day, risking my life for what? For a weekend on my host's exotic island or to save my wife's honor, I wasn't sure. As we swerved in and out of the massive traffic jams, I noticed there was an extra helmet hanging below my butt on the right side of the cycle. I kept trying to reach it so I could put it on, not being told to wear it before we left. I kept leaning to that side in order to reach, not knowing I was tilting the bike This made it difficult for Flavio to maneuver his machine and we damn near crashed. This was one of the scariest episodes of my, then, young life. I promised myself that I would never, under any circumstance, get on a motorcycle again.

As we turned the corner toward the tiny airstrip, leaning at forty-five degrees, we came to a skidding stop just in time to see the small Cessna winging it's way above Rio harbor. I had missed the flight. Flavio offered to take me back to the Pitanguy estate but I thanked him politely and took a taxi. When I returned, Marilou, the wife, informed me that we would have to go by auto the next morning. This would take about two hours and involve a ferry ride to the island. When we arrived around noon on Saturday, Ivo and Mary had just returned from scuba diving, having had a wonderful time with out us. Mary's accounting of the night before was interesting. She was supposed to spend the night in the main house where Ivo sleeps, and

Celsius, the twelve-year-old, who looked like a young Suma wrestler and weighed two hundred and fifty pounds, was to sleep in the guest-houses alone. Shannon declined the offer and slept in the guesthouse with Celsius.

PROFESSOR MARIO GONZALES ULLOA

Mario Gonzales Ulloa, the professor from Mexico City was not of pure Spanish decent. He was more of the Aztec or Indian flavor. A charming well educated, and attractive man who taught and performed procedures that was by most standards quite radical. When asked about liability in case of untoward results he said, "My patients don't bother me. If they complain I have them arrested." This gives some idea of his power and influence in his community. He was a patron of the arts and when he discovered a good, young painter whose work he liked, he would purchase his entire production and store them away to appreciate in value. He owned one of the world's best and largest collections of timepieces. His artistic sense and values influenced his work a great deal. He lectured on how important it is to take special care not to create deformity in the vaginal area because as he said, "At the moment", "it would be very detrimental to making love".

BOGUS PROFESSOR

This professor appeared at the Baker and Gordon symposium, one year, as Professor Pedro Gonzales from Madrid, Spain. At the beginning he appeared very professional and legitimate and had done his homework enough to know some of the plastic surgery literature. This posture gave him enough credibility that we all listened intently as he began his presentation. He mentioned some of the research and clinical practices that were going on in Spain. In the field of anesthesia, he reported that they were employing a new technique to determine whether or not a patient was adequately sedated enough to begin the operation. The technique was for the anesthetist to place his little finger of the right hand into the patient's nostril and pull. If the patient was heard to say, "Please take your finger out of my nose." then you could know that there was a need for more anesthesia. The audience began looking at each other and mumbling, "What! Who is this guy?" Then he said in a somewhat exaggerated Spanish accent, "I have learned that in this ah' country you have trouble with the malpractice. In ah' Spain we don't have malpractice because in ah' Spain we have guns." Dr. Gonzales described some of his patients: One was an elderly woman who needed a face lift so bad that her ear lobes were down around her hips and she had so many wrinkles she looked like a Venetian blind. On an ugly scale of ten she was twenty-seven. She would not admit that she had so many wrinkles. She said she just took a nap on a chenille bed spread. She had already had too many face-lifts so we just lowered her body. Am I going too fast for you? There was a young lady that went to her hairdresser and asked for a Barbara Streisand look so he broke her nose. After that she came to me and said, "Can you help me?" I said, "Of course." We discussed quite a bit and she said she wanted to look like a famous female television star. It was quite successful because she thought she looked like Lassie. She had a particular problem because her mouth was so big that when she smiled she got lipstick on her ears. She was written up in the Spanish Medical Journal as the only woman in the world that could swallow a banana sideways. Another patient came in with the longest nose he had ever seen which he agreed to fix but one night before the surgery she rolled over in her sleep, her nose got caught in her ear, she sneezed and blew her brains out. A patient once asked about having sex in the seventies. He said it seemed OK and then she said how about the eighties. He said well if it gets much hotter than that perhaps she should just watch television.

Can you afford skiing? This is how you can know. Take a lot of one hundred-dollar bills, wad them up one at a time, and flush them down the toilet. If this doesn't bother you then you can take up skiing."

Chapter Eight

Preceptorship

I DID A General Surgery preceptorship with Dr. Earl Boehme in Westwood Village near UCLA. Boehme had been trained at the famous Lahey Clinic in Boston and then spent some time at Kern General Hospital in Bakersfield California as chief of surgery. While we were there we got a chance to follow some of his patients and he was still returning for an occasional conference. I was so impressed with his work that I asked him if I could do a preceptorship with him in LA for one year. Dr. Boehme was an incredible surgeon from whom I learned a lot. There were other things I learned, some good and some not so good. He would say, "now when you do a rectal exam on a patient try to leave them as neat as you found them." "Never spend time with your competitors because they will not refer you patients." In spite of this advise I did have friends who also were general surgeons. I was not about to brush off their friendship just because we did the same work. These competitors may not be able to do you any good but they could sure hurt you if they wanted to. The secretary in Boehme's office was British and had that wonderful accent which sounded so proper, especially on the phone. Since then I have always wanted to have an English secretary but never did. On one occasion when Dr. Boehme had lost a sizable amount of money in an oil well venture, Elizabeth put a poem on his desk that read, "The doctor fell down the well and broke his collar bone, the doctor should treat the sick and leave the well alone." The poem was cute but didn't go very far in dispelling the doctor's depression over his financial loss.

Another Boehme axiom was that sometimes it's better not to tell the patient everything. We had an executive in the Santa Monica Hospital for an inguinal hernia repair. In the course of the procedure we noted that the bulge in is groin was more than a loop of small intestine, it was a tumor originating in the colon and on exploration it was found to be so advanced that it was incurable. We then had the unpleasant duty of informing the patient and his family. Since he was a strong looking very successful businessman we elected to tell him so he could get his affairs in order. This was a mistake, because once he realized what he was told he began to cry and never stopped until he died. His family said that he had always had a fear of this eventuality and that we should not have told him.

There was another incident in which I was not sure of the value of being totally honest with the patients. After one of the many abdominal procedures that Boehme was famous for this particular patient continued to complain of postoperative abdominal pain. On X-ray it showed that one of the bowel clamps had been left in the abdominal cavity. This seems unforgivable on the part of the surgeon but when the patient has a fat abdominal wall, the surgical wound is open and the anesthesiologist allows the anesthetic to lighten, the patient can push most of his small intestine out onto the surgical table. When this happens heavy, warm cotton packs are used to cover the intestine until the abdominal muscles are relaxed by a deeper anesthetic and the intestine can be returned to it's proper place. This is very annoying to the surgeon and can lead to complications. One can see how easy this might be to forget about an instrument left deep in the cavity. This is why most OR protocols require a sponge and instrument count before the abdominal wound is closed. So Dr. Boehme elected not to admit to the patient the truth and instead told him that he thought he had an abscess that would require drainage. The patient agreed and he was scheduled at St. John's Hospital in Santa Monica as "drainage of an abdominal abscess." Before we went to the OR he rehearsed me as to what I was expected to do. After he had the abdomen open and he had hold of the clamp, on cue, I was to distract the other people in the room by calling their attention to something out the window. At that moment he removed the clamp and dropped it to the flood on his foot so there would be no sound. Later after the wound healed for the second time, the patient thanked Dr. Boehme and me for relieving his pain so dramatically. Conventional medical ethics, not to mention the legal considerations would dictate that the doctor must inform the patient of such matters. Was Boehme's way of handling this acceptable or not? I'm not sure. All I know it sure saved a lot of hassle, it solved the problem, and best of all it saved having to deal with some lawyer that would have made a mountain out of this mole hill. Some years later I had a similar but less serious complication. I had performed a hemorrhoidectomy on a fairly young lady and on the third postoperative day she complained of severe constipation. I told her that she might have a fecal impaction and if she hadn't had a bowel movement by the next day I would do a rectal exam to see if that was her problem. The next morning I found she had no success so I slipped on a surgical glove and examined her to find that I had left gauze packing in her rectum. I slipped it out into the bedpan and told her it was a fecal impaction. The next day she was very happy and told me that I had "magic fingers."

The most tragic experience I had with Dr. Boehme was the case of a seven-year-old boy, the son of a prominent producer in the music recording business. He was admitted to St. Johns Hospital in Santa Monoca for surgery to correct a small hernia and hydrocoele of his testicle. The procedure was not complicated nor was it expected to be a significant risk. However, during the induction of anesthesia he apparently was not well oxygenated and he suffered a cardiac arrest. The anesthesiologist administered cardiac resuscitation but it was not soon enough. The child's heart and lungs recovered but he had sustained cerebral damage due to lack of oxygen. He was kept on life support for several weeks but never regained consciousness. Finally the decision had to be made as to how long we should keep a young child or for that matter anyone on full life support if the patient was brain dead with a flat brain tracing. It was the most painful moment when, with the consent of his family, the life support was removed and he was allowed to die.

At the time of this tragedy in 1950 we did not have the sophisticated technology for monitoring our patients during anesthesia that we have today. It was up to the observation and skills of the anesthetist to know how well oxygenated a patient might be at a given time. We now know that the oxygen level in a patient could be as low as 50% saturation before it would show up clinically as cyanosis. It is during that period when the heart does not have adequate oxygen than it goes into ventricular fibrillation and stops beating. When that happens the heart can be restarted by electroshock if done in time. If it is not done in five to six minutes there is usually permanent brain damage creating a vegetative state, a live but comatose patient.

The child's mother and father were religious people. With the help of the catholic influence and their many famous friends in the entertainment business they created a foundation in the name of the child and raised money enough to buy, and install cardiac monitors in every operating room at Saint Johns Hospital. Today we have wonderfully sophisticated monitors that allow the anesthetist to know within seconds if the oxygen saturation drops even one percent and there is a constant electrocardiogram running.

Chapter Nine

Indio Hospital

WHILE FINISHING THE Preceptorship with Dr. Earl Boehme in Westwood I heard about an opportunity in Indio, California, a small Railroad town just east of Palm Springs. A Dr. Wilkes had owned and operated a small hospital of approximately 90 beds. It was the only hospital in Indio at the time. The emergency room was very busy with the many traffic accidents that occurred on the highway from Indio to Blyth. Dr. Wilkes had far more work to do than he could handle and was so over worked that he became addicted to the drugs he was using to help him through his days and nights. His main helper was a nurse by the name of Mickie. One evening she found him in his bathroom dead on the floor. The syringe and ampoules of the drugs he was taking were on the floor beside him. The only other physician on his staff was a General Practitioner by the name of Dr. Dannebaum. Since most of the patients through the emergency room were severe trauma. They needed help right away. I answered their call and it became a great opportunity for me. The local was somewhat in the lower end compared to the lush practices in Palm Springs but I thought I could handle that difference later. I was busy and happy.

To improve my social and recreational life I joined the Thunderbird Country Club in Rancho Mirage. It was relatively cheap costing only $800. It was there that I met a wealthy oilman by the name of George

Cameron who asked me to see his girlfriend about nausea and abdominal discomfort. She was pregnant. He had put her up in a Motel in Indio near the little hospital where I was working. She was all alone so I ask her if she would like to go with me to some friends home that evening. The friends were the Fezzlers who lived on a fruit ranch in Indio. By the end of the evening the young lady had bonded with the Fezzlers and they new all about her problem and invited her to stay with them for as long as she needed. Fezzler contacted Cameron and demanded that he pay the young lady a sizeable amount of money for her problem. Of course Cameron thought I was a party to this extortion and demanded that I perform an abortion on the lady or he would ruin me. I tried to convince him that I had nothing to do with this scheme and I refused to do an abortion for any reason. After that I began getting phone calls and visits from his detectives and lawyers. I didn't know what to do. I was young and knew that this could do serious damage to my career and I needed help. I remembered that among my show business friends there was one that had used the famous Los Angeles attorney, Gerry Geisler and agreed to call him for me. I had one visit with him and he lectured me on the subject of avoiding these kinds of situations, abortions and extortion. He then made one phone call to Cameron's attorneys and let them know he was representing me. I never heard another word from Cameron, his legal team, the girl, or the Fizzlers.

Jim Doyle and I were sharing a small house in Palm Desert with my youngest sister, Moe. Doyle was a pure Interest/Cardiologist and had neither feel nor desire to handle trauma cases. There was plenty for him to do but not in the emergency room. One evening as we were about to retreat to our little home in Palm Desert we got a call from the Highway Patrol that a doctor was needed outside of the east end of town. When we arrived the Officer lead us to an area that was secluded in the midst of a grove of Tamarisk trees. Here we found an old car with no doors or wheels setting up on blocks. To one side there was a makeshift little kitchen area. The interior of the old car had been converted to a bed. This was the home of an elderly man who had died in his bed. Next to him on a make shift table was a candle still silently burning. Here in the twilight of the day, a life had ended quietly and almost elegantly like the small flame of the candle. It was sad and depressing.

Jim Doyle and I looked at each other after we had notified the Officers that it was too late for us to help this man. We saw the sadness and the desperation that life could be in each other's faces. Jim said, "What are we doing here? Lets find a happier place to practice." "Where, I asked?" Jim said, "Lets take one of those jobs on a luxury liner ship for say, the Carnival in Rio. I thought this was a great idea and it is exactly what I did. Jim Doyle "chickened out" because he said he had to get some dental work done.

Chapter Ten

Ships Surgeon - Ss Argentina 1950

I became the Ships Surgeon on the Moore McCormack SS Argentina for the carnival in Rio. The social life aboard a luxury cruise ship was first class. The opportunities were great including the amorous experiences. If I had taken every sexual opportunity I probably wouldn't have weighed 90 pounds when the cruise was over. It was a great job and of course everyone on board knew or wanted to know the Doctor. Most of the cases were seasickness and I finally found a simple and effective treatment for that ailment. It was ginger. I was host of my own table in the dining room. Since I was young and single they placed young ladies at my table. One was a federal judge's daughter and her cousin. One evening in the midst of dinner the judge's daughter must have thought I was not giving her enough attention so she started flipping spoonfuls of water at me until my epaulettes were dripping wet. I pushed my chair back and let go a full glass of water in her face then left the table. The chief waiter happened to see the whole event and hastened to tell the captain that the young lady deserved the water bath. Of course I was dressed down for my impulsive reaction, after all she was a first class passenger not to mention the daughter of a federal judge.

The sexiest young lady aboard lost her "breast falsies" one day in the swimming pool and was never seen again for the entire cruise. This was before the days of breast implants or we could have changed her life by adding the two things she needed to become a ten. Of all the people aboard, the most interesting and fun were the entertainers. I guess I have always been attracted to showbiz folks. Had I not become a doctor I would probably have entered some phase of that business. Jim and I had the opportunity to become actors just prior to starting medical school. At that time Twentieth Century Fox Studios was casting for a film about the Sullivan brothers who were all on duty on the same ship during the war with Japan. The Japanese torpedoed their ship and all five of them were killed. We were picked to play the parts of two of the brothers. Since our first year of medical school was to start in two months we had to choose and medical school was it. I have often wondered what different lives we would have experienced.

Being "Ships Surgeon" I had to be available to all passengers at any time of the night or day. I had to leave my suite open all the time. It wasn't unusual to return to my quarters in the late evening to find someone waiting to see me about a medical problem. On one occasion when I returned to my suite I found a beautiful young woman in my bed. She was the featured singer among the entertainers.

SS ARGENTINA in Rio

Chapter Eleven

The Cleveland Clinic 1951

DURING MY INTERNSHIP at the Hospital of the Good Samaritan in Los Angeles I met Dr. Donald Effler who was the Chest Surgeon from the Cleveland Clinic. He was there visiting Good Sam's chest surgeon, Dr. John Jones whose brother was the famous abdominal surgeon at the Cleveland Clinic (Tom Jones). Dr. Effler helped me get a job there. I had to start in anesthesia, and then move into the general surgical fellowship.

Dr. Tom Jones was a small man who hired very tall residents that required him to operate standing on a stool. He was a severe taskmaster who would never small talk with the residents. During surgery he would constantly complain to his assistants: "Doctor, your hands were made for the plow. Please try to help me." During rounds to see all the post op patient there would be five or six residents following Dr. Jones and Jones would follow the resident who's floor we were on. In one instant where the group was moving rapidly the lead doctor happened to see a nurse pulling at a door to a linen closet that seemed to be stuck. As we went by he pulled the door open for her and Dr. Jones walked into the closet. It was funny but no one laughed until later. In one of the wards an orthopedic patient was in the bed next to his patient, "Are you the famous Dr. T. E. Jones? You look more like Dr. Pee Wee Jones to me." No one dared laugh.

Dr. Jones was a deadly serious man who never married and lived his life outside of the clinic at the Cleveland Athletic Club. He died of a massive coronary occlusion in the doctor's dressing room while changing to do his first case of the day. "Dr. Jones is sick, Dr. Jones is sick," shouted Eddie the attendant who for years took care of Dr. Jones in the surgical dressing room.

The casts of other characters at the clinic were Dr. Barney Crile, the son of George Crile, the founder, Rupert Turnbull, the lead abdominal surgeon, Donald Effler, Thoracic-heart surgeon and Dr. Densmore an obese thyroid surgeon. At the time before medication was available to control hyperthyroidism symptoms, surgery was required to remove an over active thyroid gland. These patients were so sensitive that any amount of anxiety could create what was called a "thyroid storm" that could be fatal. These patients usually would be admitted to the hospital several days before surgery and each morning were taken to the OR in their bed for what they were told would be more tests. No surgery was done until they got used to these procedures. Finally with a calm patient an anesthesia was given and the thyroid gland was removed. In order to expedite the operation Dr. Densmore would do the surgery with the patient still in the bed. This got to be known as "stealing the thyroid gland." After the possibility of "thyroid storm" no longer was a problem Densmore continued to perform the surgical procedure with the patient in his bed so he could rest his oversize abdomen on his side.

One of the senior fellows named Robinett wanted to be a surgeon more than anything. He just didn't have the hands and technical skill to do the work so Barney Crile finally talked him into shifting his training to internal medicine where he belonged.

The Chief of Anesthesia, Dr. Donald Hale was a wonderful man who made an unfortunate error on one of the patients I was doing. It involved a beautiful six-year-old girl who was in for a plaster cast change as part of the treatment for congenital hip dislocation. It was imperative that she not move while the old cast was off. The Orthopedic Surgeon screamed that she was moving and needed more anesthesia. At this point Dr. Hale came in and took over the case. The anesthetic was "open drop ether" now considered a primitive form with very little control of oxygen intake. He over saturated her little lungs. She had a cardiac arrest and died.

They wanted me to tell the family but I refused. It took me a long time to recover from this tragedy.

George Crile, the founder of the clinic, had an absorbing interest in comparative anatomy. He did some of the original work to confirm that all mammals had the same physiological and anatomical characteristics: heart, brain, thyroid and adrenal glands but varied in the size and function depending on what environment they lived in. He also confirmed that they all had a normal body temperature of 98.6 degrees. The whale in the ice-cold Antarctica Ocean or the lion in tropical Africa both had body temperatures of 98.6. The whale has a very large thyroid compared to the small one of the lion. Dr. Crile had a museum at the clinic with preserved specimens to show this work. It was fascinating.

Chapter Twelve

Korea With The Marines 1952

AFTER FINISHING MEDICAL school, internship and surgical training at the Cleveland Clinic I was called to active duty as a medical officer assigned to the National Naval Medical Center in Bethesda, Maryland near Washington, D.C. This Hospital served most of the members of congress. I had been there only about three months when I was assigned to be the Junior Officer-of-the-day for one 24-hour period. This was a very busy and important place. The main reception desk was manned by a naval officer with a rank of no less than a full Commander. The duty is for the full night. A junior officer is assigned there to watch and learn. As Officer of the Day and Night this Officer was in charge of the whole institution. Around eleven PM the senior officer took a coffer break and left me in charge for less than an hour. The Chief Petty Officer was at the reception counter and I sat at the Officer of the Day's desk in the back. While the Commander was away the Petty Officer came in and told me there was an elderly gentleman at the front who wanted to visit one of the patient on the orthopedic ward. I ask him to find out who he was and what was his reason for this late visit because lights were out on the ward. The Chief went back and when he returned to me he said the gentleman would not tell him his name and insisted on being allowed to go to the ward. And Sir, "I think he is fairly drunk". I sent the

Chief back to tell him that unless I knew who he was and his business I could not allow them to light up the whole ward just for him. After that the Chief reported that the man was very angry and as he left he said he was Congressman McCormick, majority leader of the house and I would hear about this in the morning. My tour of duty was up at seven the next morning. At ten minutes after seven I was ordered to the Admirals office to explain what had happened. He had already received a formal complaint from capital hill. After relating the story to the Admiral, I told him that if I had it to do over again I would logically do the same. He agreed but then lectured me on how carefully we had to be when dealing with the Congressmen because they were the ones that made the financial appropriations that supported the Navy. Within ten days I had orders to the Fleet Marines in Korea. Brother Jim got the same orders even though he had been on active duty for only a few weeks. I guess since we were twins the Congressman wanted to be sure he got the right one so both our names were on the same set of orders. I had no problem with the punishment order for me since I was single but I was damned if it was fair for Jim. He hadn't had time to even move his furniture in the rented house and his wife, Henrietta, was pregnant with her second child. I put on my dress uniform, headed to Washington, and found the officer at the Navy Department in charge of assignment of duty for Naval Officers. I explained to him what had happened and that I was there to speak about my brother who was new in the Navy. He had a pregnant wife with a small child and he hadn't been on active duty long enough to know what was going on. I had been in the Navy long enough to know lots of young medical officers at Bethesda that should be ahead of Jim with this assignment. The Commander was intrigued that anyone would come in to speak for someone else. I got his orders changed and I reported to Field Medical School at the Marine base, Camp Lejune, North Carolina. This was where medical officers go through a crash course on how to be a Marine. The days were full of classes on everything from how to clean and shoot a M1 weapon to how to dig a "Slit Trench." the classical place to hide if the enemy was near or as a toilet for the field. The toughest part was the early morning calisthenics and the cross-country hikes. It was a great experience and after some time in Korea I was very grateful for the training. There were a total of ninety doctors in my class, all of whom were scheduled to replace most of the medical officers with the First Marine Division. After reporting in with my orders, I was given my Barracks assignment. With some difficulty I managed to find my bunk and as I stood facing it I noticed on the other side a giant of a man who stood at least six feet eight inches tall. He introduces himself to me as Dr. Bill Norton and at the other bunk was an equally small fellow who couldn't have been more than five feet six inches tall. This was Dr. Willie White. As I looked at these guys I couldn't help but say to myself, "We are a bunch of freaks and they must have given us this assignment to get rid of us." It also occurred to me what a hell of a job it would be for Norton to dig his "Slit Trench." Perhaps these two could dig just one and share it

We were flown to Japan in a Pan American Clipper ship that was first class for those days. We spent a few days in Kobe at the Marine Base then flown in a Dc 3 with bucket seats to Pusan. The First Marine Division had finished their retreat from the Chosen reservoirs and started back up the peninsula toward the 38th parallel. A complement of ninety doctors was sent out to replace most of the physicians with the division. Among the group were doctors of all kind, internist, pediatricians, pathologists, etc., with only a few trained surgeons.

Awaiting assignment in Korea

I can't imagine how the Pentagon or who ever makes such decisions could think that an internist or a pediatrician could be of much use in a war. Common sense would dictate that what had to be dealt with in that setting was trauma, mega trauma. Usually people become internists because the site of blood makes them sick. What were they doing there? I guess to the "brass." a doctor is a doctor.

⁓

We arrived in Kobe, Japan and then flown over to Pusan, Korea to join the Corps. We were issued field clothing and all the gear we would need. It was in the fall and winter was on its way. We were told that it got very cold there so we carried all the warm things we could. Some of us even lugged a case of Scotch whisky because we were tipped of that the most valuable thing for barter was whisky. Not for the natives but the other branches of our service. Over the months that followed we found this to be very true. After several months just to be able to take a shower was worth a bottle of scotch to the engineering corps. They were the only ones that had the ability and equipment to create a shower.

After our arrival in Pusan at the southern tip of the Korean peninsula, we boarded open bed trucks and headed north. When we reached the mountainous area near the 38th parallel it began to rain. This made us quite miserable and to add to the chill, we began seeing interesting round objects all along the side of the road for miles and miles. We were told that these were land mines that had been freshly removed just ahead of us by the engineer corps. Soon thereafter we began hearing the sounds of heavy artillery so we knew that we were near the front line of battle. The road curved around a sizable hill into a valley. There were many tents scattered over the hillside with muddy roads heavily traveled by trucks and the ever-present jeep. This was headquarters for the First Marine Division where we were to report to the Surgeon General for our assignments. The rain had slowed down to drizzle. We all milled around or sat on our duffel bags waiting for our turn to be interviewed by the most powerful man in our life at this moment. General Pottenger held in his hands our destiny. He could assign us either to the battalion aid station right at the front line or back to one of the division hospitals, a much safer place. The odds of being killed at the battalion aid station were very high. At this assignment, the doctor, called "Medic" was expected to accompany the Coremen out between the line of fire to retrieve wounded Marines. It was almost like a death sentence. Of course the best assignment of all was back to the holding hospital unit where most if not all of the heavy surgery was done on the seriously wounded. Because I had been trained in general surgery at the Cleveland Clinic with lots of trauma experience in the emergency rooms, I was assigned to "E" Med, a mobile hospital. This was forty or fifty miles behind the line. Because of the "E" it was always referred to as "Easy Med." When I arrived I was immediately made chief of surgery because of my training in general surgery. Even though I was only a Lieutenant junior grade I had full Commanders and in one instance a Navy Captain assist me in the OR. These were career Naval officers among whom rank meant more that skill and training. When it came to opening a severely wounded abdomen or chest they seemed to know when to defer. Months later,

I ran into one of the internist who had been assigned to the battalion aid station. He looked terrible and had been sent back to our holding hospital on a psychiatric disability. Diagnosis: chronic stress disorder once called "battle fatigue" or "shell shock." What it meant was that he simply couldn't take it any more. I had often felt some element of guilt that I had been lucky enough to have chosen surgery as a specialty and even luckier to have been sent back rather than forward to the Battalion Aid Station near the front line. The first thing he said to me was, "where were you assigned to duty by the Surgeon General?" I said, "Easy Med." He replied in a somber tone with tears in his eyes, "I was assigned to "Hard Med." A week later he was sent home.

There were many times while making rounds in the hospital tents that the wounds of a Marine would be borderline in severity. A decision would have to be made as to whether or not he should be sent back to his battalion or evacuated back to a holding unit. Even if the wounds were severe enough it might be justified to send him to one of the Naval hospitals in Japan. After that, he might be lucky enough to be transferred back to the states. On one occasion while examining the relatively minor wounds of a young Marine who knew he would more than likely be sent back to full duty with his battalion said, "Doc, do you realize what power you have? You could send me back or even home if you would, and probably save my life." As I pondered his statement, I realized what an awesome responsibility I had been given. My reply to him was that I would love nothing better than to send every American soldier and Marine home but I had to do my job the best I could without getting emotionally involved. If a doctor allowed himself to suffer with each patient, he would die a little with every one he lost until he would be useless.

One of the most bizarre wounds I encountered during the Korean War involved a marine who was wounded by "trip flare." Often wires would be strung between the battle lines about a foot off the ground that were connected to trip flares. When the wire was tripped during the night it detonated a charge that blew and ignited a magnesium or heavy metal flare into the air. A small parachute allowed the flare to descend slowly and to light up the area so the enemy could be seen and "neutralized." On this occasion the marine trip one of these flares accidentally and it happened to be just beneath him. The flare struck him in the anal area and embedded totally into his rectum. Of course it burned fully inside his pelvis. He was evacuated by helicopter immediately to our medical unit and when I saw him right away he was fully conscious and alert. He said, "Doc, it was a trip flare, it went right up my ass. Can you get it out?" I said, "Are you sure?" He replied, "Yes, it was like I was a human rocket, fire shot out of my ass, I couldn't believe it!" He appeared to be in very little pain, his vital signs were normal and he was quite cheerful. After starting an intravenous and preparing universal donor blood for transfusion and some sedation was given. The area was prepped. I put on sterile gloves and explored the rectal wound. As my hand penetrated his pelvis up to the level of my wrist, I could feel the metal part of the flare. It was still warm. I eased what I could out carefully, knowing that this could cause sudden severe bleeding. The wound had been burned so severely that the tissue was cauterized and at that moment there was no significant bleeding. Not being acquainted with these flares, I thought I had removed the whole thing. I knew he was in need of major surgery to create a colostomy that brings the upper colon out through an opening in the abdominal wall to prevent the feces from entering the openings in the pelvic structures. If his general condition stayed good a debridement of the wound would be necessary to remove as much of the damaged area as possible that would probably require cleaning out most of the organs in the pelvis including bladder and rectum. I knew his chances of survival were slim because even if he withstood the surgery, the absorption of heavy metal from the flare would probably kill him. He was evacuated by helicopter to the large army hospital in Soul. This was the nearest facility that had x-ray capability and the films showed the entire parachute still imbedded in his abdomen. It was futile to think he could survive such a horrendous trauma. He died the next day.

The winter in Korea was bitter and miserable, specially living in a tent. Even though the engineer corps "strong backed" these floppy structures and Installed a wooden floor with a potbelly stove in the center, it was far from the comforts of home. My cot was in the middle of the tent near a table that was used for meals, writing letters home and worst of all for playing cards. It just so happened that in my medical company there were four doctors that were Bridge fanatics. During a lull in the war there would be time to rest, read, and sometimes enjoy games. The' Bridge game was, however, a seemingly endless one. It would go on into the wee hours of the morning. The hooded light that hung over the table shined into my eyes, so I found it very difficult to sleep. I pleaded with them on many occasions to limit their time and put a curfew on the game so everyone in the tent could get some sleep. I was ignored until one night I took my forty-five handgun out from under my pillow and blew out the light. It was only then that these "bridge nicks" paid any attention to me. I have hated the game of Bridge ever since and to this day I can't stand the sight of a deck of cards.

A visit by the reporters from the Cleveland Chronicle newspaper was accompanied by a large carton of blood donated by citizens of Cleveland. Their story was to follow the Cleveland blood to the battle-field in hopes it would find it's way into some Marines from Cleveland. This was fairly easy but when they discovered a surgeon who trained at The Cleveland Clinic who could administer the transfusions their loop was complete. However, when they returned and the story was published it was so fictionalized I didn't recognize it. The story was good enough on it's own merit and didn't need the phony drama they added. This was fairly common with all of the reporting about the Korean War. The only magazine that seemed to consistently report what was really happening was "U.S.News and World Report.

"One of my fondest memories of the Korea experience was the children. There were many orphaned by the war and when we were fartherest from the battle line we would take them in to our camp, feed and care for them. One of our favorites was an eight-year-old boy that was given the name of "Pisspot." He wore a visor cap with his name printed on the turned up bill. He became the major mascot of our company. One day we had an unannounced inspection visit by the Marine General. He liked our taking care of the children but he wasn't sure we should give them such names. He gave us the news that we were ordered to move up to the front within artillery range and we could not take the children with us. The departure was sad like leaving our families behind but we knew it was best. We moved our medical company, "E Med" up in a valley so close to the enemy that our own artillery interfered with our OR lights. It became so bad at one time we had to transfer our power source to the Jeeps and other Vehicles.

Two months later in the spring and after a light rain we noticed a group of people walking along the winding road above our valley. As they descended into our camp we realize these were all our children. They had found us after walking some thirty miles. You can imagine the home coming celebration that we enjoyed. "Pisspot" was the head of the pack.

Chapter Thirteen

The Eleventh Finger Plan

AFTER FINISHING MY tour of duty in Korea I had orders to report to the Marine Recruit Depot in San Diego, Calif. At about the same time brother, Jim had orders to the Fleet Marines in Korea again. By this time Jim and Henrietta had two children and were expecting another. I couldn't see him leaving his family and taking the risk in that crazy war. We came up with a plan. Even though I hated the idea I agreed to switch orders with him and go back for another year in Korea. After all it would be a good deal for the Marines since they would be getting a seasoned combat doctor with experience. We know it might be considered some kind of a crime like impersonating an officer or who knows but we were sure we could pull it off. We were twins and looked enough alike that we felt no one could tell the difference. I would become Jim and Jim would become John. The only way we might be discovered could be the thumb finger print that was always required when receiving pay. We knew this would not be a problem for me because no one in overseas combat was ever paid. The money just accumulates until you are back in the states then the back pay could be claimed. However it could be a problem for Jim so we thought of a cunning way to solve it. We would go to a friendly dental officer who would make a cast of out thumb fingers and create a duplicate in neoprene rubber. I would carry his fake finger and he

would carry mine. When signing the paycheck it would be no problem to palm the mock finger and apply it to the document at hand
(no pun intended). As we were on terminal leave before reporting to
our new assignments and about to make the switch Jim received a
change in his orders requiring him to report back to the Dahlgren,
Virginia Naval Proving Base where he had developed a fun and valuable friendly relationship with the commanding Admiral. They had
done a lot of fishing together and the Admiral didn't want to lose his
buddy so he had his orders changed for a second tour of duty under
his command. Of course this was a great relief for me because I really
didn't want to repeat the war experience that I had been lucky enough
to survive. However, I would have done it to save my brother (what a
guy! "He's not heavy he's my brother").

As ordered I reported to the Marine Recruit Depot in San Diego
where they gave me an easy assignment as the team doctor for the
Marine football team. I guess since I had returned from an experience
in hell, they would reward me with an easy job. The team was made
up of some of the best players from both college and the professionals.
As a matter of fact a good number of players had contracts to play
with the pro when their service duty was completed. (Notice these
guys were too valuable to send to combat) Some of our finest players,
especially the running backs were black guys. One in particular was
the best I have seen anywhere. He was truly our secret weapon. There
was a conference made up of five or six teams from other branches
of the service that played for the championship. The best team other
than our Marines was the Naval Air Base. One game on our schedule
was the Brook Army Medical in San Antonio, Texas. All of our games,
like the pros, were played on Sundays. The college teams always were
on Saturday. We were free on Saturday so our coach took the whole
team to see the game between TCU and Alabama in Fort Worth. He
got a block of very good seats about half way up on the fifty-yard line.

As we settled in our seats and the grand stand began to fill we noticed some rumbling from the crowd around us. This got louder and louder until our coach asks someone, "What's the matter?" The fans started yelling, "We don't want those niggers setting up here." The coach said, "Where should they sit?" The reply was, "In the end zone." Now our guys began to rumble telling the white fans that we were a football team who came to gather and we intended to see the game together. The argument grew louder and more heated until it was on the verge of a riot. Our black players solved the ruckus by saying, "Look guys we're used to this and we don't want you to get in a fight over us. We'll go to the end zone." They all got up and left to go sit in a make shift bleacher in the end of the field. I had always been proud to be a Texan but on this occasion I was ashamed and so angry there were tears in my eyes. The next day we played our game against the all white Brook Army team. We beat them so badly it was a joke.

Chapter Fourteen

New Office In Beverly Hills 1953

POLICE SURGEON
MOVIE COMPANY THE SWAN
GRACE KELLY / ALEC GUINNESS

LATE SUMMER OF 1955 I was on a flight returning from Europe when I happened to get seated next to an attractive young lady. In the course of our conversation, I learned that she worked as secretary for a film director at MGM by the name of Charles Vidor. She was excited about the possibility that she might be able to accompany him on location. The picture was "The Swan" and the cast consisted of Grace Kelly, Alex Guinness, Louis Jordan, Jessie Royce Landis, and Estelle Winwood. She also mentioned that MGM liked to send a doctor along on these location shoots and that they often had difficulties finding one. The filming was to be for the most part done at the Biltmore House in Ashville, North Carolina. This was a replica of a Lori Chateau brought over and had reconstructed by George Vanderbilt in the 1890s. It has been said that this is the largest mansion in the United States with some fifty-seven rooms. When I got back to Beverly Hills I found that my new office on Roxbury Dr. was not yet completed and that it would require at least another two months before I could see patients there. What could I do for two more months? Then I remembered the conversation on the plane. Perhaps I could take the job with MGM if they were indeed still looking for a physician. When I called the studio they said I was the answer their prayer, and I was delighted to have a new adventure, especially one that would allow me to meet and get to know Grace Kelly. The crew and set designers went to the location one month before the principals in order to prepare the sets and the restoration of buggies, carriages and the castle. I accompanied them, lived in the same hotel with them and joined them at the castle for lunches. They became my friends and I enjoyed watching them do their magic work. I set up my clinic in the lower hillside floor of the castle and believe me with the horses and carriage work I had plenty of patients. When the actors and filmmakers arrived there suddenly appeared white tablecloths, silver, china and all the elegance of a fine hotel. The crew and I had been eating our lunches on the bare picnic tables like campers. Suddenly I was confused as to where I belonged in this "pecking order." I didn't want to abandon by crew friends and suddenly become too important to lunch with them any more, so I asked them what I should do. They said they thought as the physician for the company I definitely belonged at the white tablecloths and they would understand. So with my friend's encouragement, at the first lunch, I boldly chose a seat next to Grace Kelly. Of course everyone wanted to know who I was. When I told them I suddenly became accepted as an important member of the crew. My first patient was the director himself, Charles Vidor. He was a bit of a hypochondriac and required almost daily medical attention. Grace developed a mild upper respiratory infection and required visits to my clinic almost every day for Antibiotic injections. When Alex discovered me he requested that I make a "house call" to his hotel suite every evening. We always had a Scotch and wonderful conversation. Alex was a charming and incredibly talented man. I treasured those cocktail hours that I was lucky enough to spend with him.

One evening Grace had a cocktail party in her suite for the cast and I was invited. She asked me to open a bottle of champagne. As is well known the cork can become a missile so instead of just covering the cork with a napkin I simple aimed it toward a wall. The cork hit the wall then the ceiling and then Grace's head. Fortunately it had lost some of its power by the time it hit Grace and she wasn't hurt. Everyone including Grace thought it was funny.

By the time the company returned to Los Angeles I knew the principals very well. Of course outside of medical attention I was most interested in Grace and Alex Guinness seemed to be most interested in me. He was staying at the Beverly Hill Hotel and Grace was renting the home of Gaylord Houser.

During our many cocktail hour conversations I had mentioned to Alex my interest in Palm Springs and that my sister, Moe had rented a house there for the season. He expressed an interest since he had long heard that this was the "Play ground" for movie people. We loosely agreed that I would take him there some weekend when the schedule allowed. He settled on a date and I was to meet him in front of the hotel and drive him there for the weekend. It just so happened to be the weekend that Grace had scheduled a party at the Gaylord house on that Saturday. I was so interested in Grace and we had a few dates for dinner, I completely forgot my appointment with Alex. During the party someone asked where Alex was and a friend of his said he was gone to Palm Springs. I said, "NO, I was supposed to take him there." The friend said, "OH my God you were the one who stood him up. He waited for you for over two hours. He was very upset. Send him some flowers or something." What a GOOF!

After the film was almost finished it was around Christmas and Grace went home to Philadelphia for the holiday. Prince Rainier came there for Christmas and asked Grace's father for her hand in marriage. It was news in all the tabloids that she had accepted his proposal, and Grace was to become a princess.

She returned to Los Angeles shortly thereafter to finish work on the film. She called me to make a house call and needed some medication for another mild upper respiratory infection. While there she showed me a lot of candid photographs she had taken while in Ashville during the filming. I congratulated her on her engagement, and then I asked, "Do you love him?" Her response was, "He's awfully nice."

By this time Dr. Jim had found a place to practice as a family doctor in Yuba City/Marysville, California. He picked the location by the Game Map. He figured that he could choose most any place, why not one that had good hunting and fishing. This area north west of Sacramento was perfect. He joined a Dr. Hamilton who was looking for an associate. He raised his five children there with his wife Henrietta. His extra training in surgery made him a fine asset to the community.

During my training with Dr. Albert Davis in San Francisco, I was able to visit him and his family on some weekends. I arrived on Friday around ten o'clock on one occasion. I was tired and needed some rest. At four o'clock the next morning he shook me awake and said, "wake up, wake up, we've got to go before day light." Where are we going? "Duck Hunting." He practically dressed me and before I was half awake we were in the car. It was pitch dark. The dogs were in the back seat licking my neck. It was cold and miserable. By the time we got into the duck blinds and up to our asses in water, a light rain started. Jim said, "Great, the ducks come in low in the rain." I said, "Are we having fun?" He said, "be quiet, you'll scare the ducks away." About that time two ducks came in low and I fired two shot. I accidentally got both of them. Jim raved on about how incredible it was that I "got a double" the first time duck hunting. The light rain stopped, the sun came out and it was a beautiful morning. Jim was angry and said, "It's a damn 'Blue Bird day' now and we won't see anymore ducks today." The next time I paid a visit I made sure it wasn't in duck season.

Chapter Fifteen

Marriage 2
Eva Gabor

AFTER MY FIRST brief venture into matrimony, I didn't come close to trying it again for almost ten years. The second wife was Eva Gabor. I met her in Palm Springs at the famous Racquet Club. I had

EVA GABOR

gone there to spend some time with Millie Considine, a good friend from New York. She was the wife of Bob Considine a well-known columnist for the Hearst Newspapers.

Bob had to travel all over the world for the newspaper and Millie was left, on many occasions, without an escort. She knew many prominent people that included lots of folks in show business. When in the Los Angeles she was often invited to social events and parties. Because I was single and loose she frequently asked me to be her escort. For a young doctor, being with Millie was good PR because she introduced me to many people. One was Eva Gabor. We experience some chemistry between us so I began dating her. Eva was an incredibly sweet lady and her beauty along with her sisters was well known. How could I resist? Soon after we met she was scheduled to do a play in New York with Regional Gardner called "The Little Glass Clock." It was a period, French farce. Eva asked me to come for the opening and experience the birth of a "hit play" on Broadway. This was a new world to me and I was fascinated by what happened. After the final curtain a party was held at mother, Jolie's home to await the early morning edition of newspapers to read the critics review of the play. They were all bad. The mood of the party turned to resemble a "wake." One would think the crowd had a collective death in their families at once. For the first time I learned how, after long rehearsals and hard work, the drama critics could kill a play with unflattering reviews.

After a few days of recovering from her dreadful depression caused by the death of her play, Eva said, "Darling since the play failed I don't have anything to do. So, why don't we get married?" So on a cold winters day in Eva's town house on Fifth Avenue, New York we were married by a judge who suffered from the most acute attack of "stage fright" I had ever seen. I could understand how this might happen because most of the invited guests were among the most powerful and important people in New York society.

Of course my twin brother, Jim was best man. When I asked him what he thought about my marrying Eva. His reply was, "I guess there should be at least one Gabor in everyman's life."

We spent our brief honeymoon at Jolie's house in Connecticut then headed west to Beverly Hills. We found a house to rent in the hills above the Beverly Hills Hotel. The owner was Tony Douchette, an artist and movie set designer. The home was built on a hillside with the main entrance and living room the top floor and the bedrooms below. The interior was beautiful but outrageous. The living room had two story high ceilings; large windows covered by long luxurious drapes, huge sunbursts paintings on the walls (Douchette was famous for his sun burst designs) and a chandelier to end all chandeliers. It was huge, made of glass crystal with what appeared to be a thousand flowers, and birds flying in all direction. On one of the many occasions that Eva was away I took a friend of mine through the house. As we sat in the dramatic living room for a cocktail, I asked him what he thought of the place. He looked around, rolled his eyes stroked his chin and said, "It's sort of like looking up Alice in Wonderland's ass."

I was just starting in general surgery and joined the practice of an elderly doctor by the name of Dr. Charles F. Nelson. He had a big practice in Beverly Hills but didn't like surgery. It was great for me because he referred all of those cases. Dr. Nelson had a theory that everyone was deficient in Calcium because they couldn't absorb it from their intestinal tract. His solution was to give it intravenously. Patients would come in twice a month for the injections. At times there would be six or seven people lying in his treatment rooms at the same time getting their I.V. Calcium. His colleagues often referred to him Dr.C. F. Nelson as Dr. "Calcium Fixation Nelson."

At this time Eva was away touring with Noel Coward's play, "Blyth Spirit"." After that she got the sitcom, "Green Acres" with Eddie Albert. Her theatrical dresser (maid) was a sweet Cockney lady she picked up while doing a play in London. Dottie had poorly fitting dentures that clicked when she tried to talk. The other members of the household were two dogs: a tiny Yorkshire, named Sonny and a beautiful standard, gray poodle named Delilah. It wasn't long until I realized my place in the hierarchy of our home and marriage. I ranked somewhere between Dottie and Delilah. Sonny didn't matter much because he was so small and always traveled with Eva. This left Delilah and me home alone so we made the best of it and became good friends.

As I became busier and had many patients in the hospital I naturally got lots of phone calls at night. Eva was doing the TV show and had early calls so she needed her sleep. She asked me if I would take the phone out of the bedroom. I told her that if it left the room then

I would have to go with it. So I was banished to the guest room. It was uniquely furnished with an authentic Russian slay made into a bed. It was hard to get into, requiring a stool or an athletic jump. The only thing good about this was that Delilah came with me to keep me company.

When it came time to deal with the finances of our marriage the problems began. It revolved around tax time. Eva was doing very well financially making at least four times as much as I was. She asked me to pay all of the income taxes, hers and mine. I explained to her with the accountant's help, that if I did that I would have little or nothing left. Besides she had most of the deductions that I could not take. She was very upset about my attitude and said, "Darling the man should take care of all of his wife's expenses including the taxes." Her mother, Jolie always referred to me as "that poor little doctor that married my Eva." She had violated one of her mother's cardinal rules: "you must always marry a rich man."

The marriage lasted just about a year and when people began referring to me as Dr. Gabor I knew it was time to leave. Life with Eva was like living in a comic strip. Shortly after I moved out, Eva called me at my office and said, "Darling, we should never have gotten married we should have just lived together."

Since I had the audacity to divorce a Gabor, I was stricken from the list of people in their social world and did not see Eva again for ten years. By this time I had an office on the seventh floor of a highrise in Century City. One afternoon I was on the elevator returning to my office. The elevator door opened and Eva stepped on. I said, "Hello Eva." She gave me a bewildered look, cocked her head and said, "Do I know you?" I said, "I don't think so but I was once married to you." She was silent for a moment then said, "My God is that you John? You look so good I didn't recognize you. Who does your Plastic Surgery?"

Chapter Sixteen

Francis Benedum

MARRIAGE 3
BAILEY MY 2ND SON BORN

FRAN BENNET

LEAVING EVA I moved into an apartment with my sister, Moe on Beverly Glen. After several months I met wife number three. An old friend, Jim Philips called me one evening and asked me to join him at 351 South Fuller Avenue, Apartment 6 L in Park LaBrea. His girl friend had a new roommate from Texas that was without a date. I joined them. She was one of the most beautiful women I had ever met. Her Texas drawl reminded me of my days at Texas Tech. I thought: here was a lovely young lady from my home state of Texas; perhaps it was meant to be. Little did I know? Her name was Fran Bennett (changed for her movie career from

79

Francis Benedum). She had been in Los Angeles for about two year and had already done fifty some television shows and a movie with Liz Taylor, Rock Hudson, and James Dean by the name of "Giant." Fran knew all of these people quite well, especially James Dean. Soon after I started dating her Dean was killed in an auto wreck on the way to Santa Barbara. Among others in the building were Charlton Heston and a special guy that became a close and dear friend, the great tennis player, Tony Trabert. He lived on the first floor of our high-rise with his wife and two children Brooke and Mike. The wife was a successful model who became obsessed with her body weight and was probably bulimic. She became so thin that one day Tony told her that going to bed with her was like going to bed with a bicycle. This and other incompatibilities regarding her career finally lead to divorce.

As Fran and I became more serious and talked about getting married, I thought I should do something about my marriage to Eva Gabor. For a man to divorce a Gabor was definitely against their rules. They were supposed to file the action, get the divorce along with all the assets. Since my assets were meager I was definitely on the Gabor black list. The quickest way I could divorce was to live in Nevada for six months to qualify as a resident of that state. I got a job as a house physician at the Washoe Medical Center in Reno. During that time I wrote letters to Fran almost daily.

I was so crazy about her that I didn't really get to know her. This was the pattern of my life. The first marriage was something I had to do; the old "shotgun marriage" for ten days and as for Eva Gabor; what guy could turn down such and opportunity. It was an experience I had to have. So here I was "in love" for the first time.

Fran's family was very social in Ft. Worth, Texas. They were prominent at the Country Club and she was a Junior Leager. Her mother's family was in the grain business that was run by her grand father, Frank Bailey and her uncle Frank Bailey Jr. There must have been a gene missing from the women's XX chromosomes because they were all crazy the same way. Everything in their physical surroundings was clutter and chaos. Grandmother Bailey's upstairs living quarters was so full of trash and clothes all over the floor she had developed trails and tunnels to get to the bed and bathroom. While in Fort Worth for our wedding I stayed at the grandparents home in what I suppose was the guest room down stairs. I was told that I could never go up stairs. So naturally I took the first opportunity when no one was around to see what was upstairs. She saved everything even the skin from slices of baloney, putting the stringy stuff in the freezer with the ice cubes. Every closet in the house was stuffed. When I was ready to go to bed there was no place to hang up my clothes so I left them on the floor. Every place in the house was full of junk, even under the beds. Fran's mother, Gege was the same and so was Fran. The men of the family were all fairly normal. Grandfather Bailey faked deafness so he wouldn't have to respond to his wife's constant babble about herself. She told me that no one had ever said a bad thing about her in her whole life and that she had never looked at herself in the mirror when she was nude. Frank Jr. was a fine gentleman, friendly, intelligent, well organized and very tolerant of his mother's and his sister's obvious mental illnesses. We had a big fancy wedding for the benefit of the family because Fran and I had already been married in Phoenix with a Justice of the Peace in a tiny ceremony. My sister, Frankie and her husband, Hal Jones stood up for us. After the wedding we returned to L.A. to live in Fran's apartment at Park La Brea. Shortly there after I began to notice some "quirks" in my new wife's behavior, like making small decisions. She couldn't seem to make up her mind about anything. One evening we were driving to a restaurant I had chosen for dinner. We had parked the car and were walking toward the restaurant; she suddenly let me know that she didn't want to go there. I said, "OK where would you like to go?" The one I had chosen happened to be Chinese. I said, would you like, Italian." No! "How about a nice French"? No! "Well tell me what you want." "I don' know" This went on for at least an hour and I still could not get her to decide what she wanted to eat. I said, "maybe you aren't hungry so lets don't have dinner." "No", she said, "I'm starving" She then she sat down on the curb and wouldn't move for half an hour. I begged her to either make up her mind or we would just go home. After I threatened to leave her there sitting on the curb, she finally went back to the car and we returned home. This was the story of her life.

On her birthday Tony Trabert and I planned a surprise party for her. I had told her that I was taking her to a fancy restaurant but we were stopping by the Trabert apartment for a drink on the way. She said no. She didn't want to stop there. The apartment was crowed with her friends so I physically dragged her to the door and pushed her in. Of course she was happy once she knew what was happening. Life with Fran was not easy but there were some good times. She was a beautiful young woman and a very good actress. She got almost every job she tried out for but as one producer told, "Fran you could get any job we had in the first few minutes of an interview but if you stayed twenty more minutes you would loose it because you started telling us how to direct the picture."

After a few months Fran became pregnant so we moved from Park Labra to a small house at 9156 Warbler Place in Los Angeles just north of Beverly Hills. It was an interesting neighborhood. Rock Hudson and his wife, Phyllis lived across the street to the right and a big family, the Weirs with lots of red headed kids lived directly across the street. It was about that time we learned that our neighbor; Mr. Hudson had let it be known that he was gay.

When we moved I was still practicing general surgery with offices at 435 North Roxbury Drive in Beverly Hills. On September 16, 1958 our son, Bailey was born at the Doctors Hospital on the corner of Beverly Glen and Santa Monica Boulevard. The hospital failed and was later torn down.

Bailey

Sweets and Bailey

I had custody of Bailey since he was four years old. He was a very important big brother to Sean and Kelli. He was a very good student and always wanted to be a part of the film business as writer/director.

When Bailey graduated from high school he went to Carnage Mellon University film school in Pittsburgh. He made the dean's list his first year and was so eager to launch his career and thought he knew enough, he dropped out and came home to Hollywood.

We were living in Bel Air at the time and the Hippy era was on. He had grown a beard, long hair and dressed like a typical homeless character. He decided to make an "under ground movie". It was indeed underground in the subterranean sewer beneath UCLA. He came home late one afternoon. There was no one home and he had no key with him. He tried to get a window open in the front of the house but no luck. Larry Flint lived across the street with his two body-guards on constant duty. They saw him trying to "break in" the house, came over, pinned him to the wall with their guns and threatened to call the police. Bailey tried desperately to convince them that he lived there. They said, "Yeah you look like you live here". Fortunately after they had him scared out of his wits I happened to arrive home and convinced them he was my son and did live there. Bailey immediately went up to his room shaved his beard and changed his clothes to a clean-cut preppie and his Hippy days were over.

Bailey went on to create his own company that developed software designed to manage e-mail. He invested some money he had inherited from his mother's estate. His portfolio was made up entirely of tech stocks that grew to around seven million dollars. I suggested that he take at least five million off the table and go with the rest. He did consider this but since he thought the tech revolution was here to stay, he didn't want to do it. He rode the decline in tech stocks until he had lost over 90%. Needless to say he was devastated and I don't think he has fully recovered to this day.

At that time I was working as a police surgeon at the Los Angeles Receiving Hospital. There were very few emergency hospitals in those days so the city of Los Angeles furnished one with ambulance service to bring in accident victims. The only patients that were admitted for inhouse care were policemen. Other patients needing hospitalization were transferred to LA County. I worked the evening shift from four to twelve pm so I could have the early part of the day for my private practice. There usually were four or five of us doctors there on each shift and with eight treatment rooms we were kept very busy. Each doctor had a color code light on the door so the nurses could let us know when the next patient was ready. One day I noticed that on certain occasions my light would come on immediately after I had finished and that there may be two or more other doctors available and just sitting in the hall way. Finally I asked why this happened. A nurse named Agnes said, "Haven't you notice that each time we do this your next patient would usually be a child or someone with facial lacerations." "No I replied, I hadn't noticed." She then said, "Why don't you go into the room with some of the other doctors and see how poorly they repaired lacerations. They do not freshen the wounds well (debridmont) and then they sew it up with large silk. You use fine nylon. As a matter of fact I think you're in the wrong specialty. You should be in Plastic Surgery not General Surgery." I had never considered Plastic Surgery but after this nurses observation, I began reading everything I could about the specialty and became fascinated by the difference. This was surgery that most of the patients wanted. It was creative. The patients were not critically ill and they paid in advance. I became so convinced that what nurse, Aggie had said to me was right that I decided to quit General Surgery and take two more years of training in that field. I applied to several places and decided on a preceptorship with Doctor Albert Davis in San Francisco. One of the books that really excited me was two-volume co-written by Sir Harold Guilles of England and Dr Ralph Millard of Miami. Millard had spent two years with Guilles putting the material together that covered how Plastic and Reconstructive Surgery had become important in repairing the awful injuries resulting from World War one and two. The trench warfare of world war one had yielded numerous facial wounds. Dr. Guilles was an ear, nose and throat specialist that was the closest specialty to Reconstructive Surgery at the time. He rose to the occasion and became what many consider to be the father of modern plastic surgery. There were so many facial deformities that a special hospital was created in the outskirts of London. It was called Rocksdown House. These wounds frequently required tissue transfer from other parts of the body. Guilles created and used the "tubed pedicle" for that purpose along with skin grafts. During staged procedures these ambulatory patients would come and go to

Rocksdown House. Their group was called the "Guineypig Club." I chose Dr. Davis because he had worked with Dr. Guilles in London as a trainee.

When I told Fran about my plan and suggested to her that she would have to move to San Francisco she said, "I can't leave. What about my career? I have to be in Los Angeles so I can go on interviews." So we agreed that I would go alone and she and the baby, Bailey would remain in LA and I could come down on weekends. After all it wouldn't be forever, just two years and we were young. I was so excited about what this meant for our future that I agreed to her terms. Fran then decided to move out of our small house on Warbler Place and rented Shelly Winters home in Beverly Hills. As the months went by and I became more dedicated to my new learning environment Fran began living like a single person. The maid who seemed to like me and was concerned about our marriage finally told me that Fran had been entertaining other men and at one time had a Texas ex-football player named Bubba living there with her. On Baileys second birthday September 16, 1960 she had a birthday party for him. There was a clown and all the stuff that goes with a two-year-old little boy's birthday. Of course I came down for the occasion. While there I confronted her with information I had received from the maid. Naturally she denied everything. Since she was not doing any work and didn't seem to want to, I insisted that she come live with me in SF for the remainder of my training so I could spend time with my little son. She refused to even consider it so a short time later while she was back in Texas I moved her clothes and all with the baby to my apartment in San Francisco. When she found out what I had done she went crazy and demanded that I move the baby and all her things back to LA. I refused so she came and did it herself. Not wanting to get physical there wasn't much I could do. She smoked and began drinking too much. Finally moved back to Texas where the money was. She continued to live in "Tinsel town" on occasions where her career died.

Fran's real father left her mother, Gege when she was an infant. She never knew him. Gege married a second time to a man by the name of Darwin Benedum. I never met this stepfather in any of my visits because he was always in the hospital with some incurable disease. Darwin never adopted Fran but she used his name. Gege had a son by him named Mike who was about two years younger than Fran. Darwin died a few months after I became involved with this family. His uncle Benedum was an immensely wealthy oilman. His home was a huge old, palatial estate in the most elegant suburb of Pittsburgh. Mr. Benedum, age ninety something died a few months after Darwin had passed. His estate was worth more than one hundred million dollars. Gege and Mike were heirs through Darwin so they were invited to Pittsburgh for the reading of the will. Gege wanted Fran and me to accompany her for the occasion. The idea of being present at the reading of a will such as this was fascinating. I had only seen this in the movies. All of his heirs amounted to only five or six people. The old man never had any children so all of the people there were nieces or nephews. The reading was held in the library of old world decor, large, dark and somber as the occasion. The attorney who read the will was very serious and would have gotten the part had this really been a movie. Fran was not mentioned because she was not an "issue of body" or married to one. Gege and Mike definitely qualified. The first part of the will stipulated that the estate would be divided in half. The first half would go to specified charities and taxes. The remaining residue would go to his heirs. Gege and Mike came away with about ten million dollars. Fran was disappointed because she thought she should have received something but she didn't. She would have to wait until her mother died before she would receive anything and this gave her mother total control of her for the rest of Gege's life. Fran's brother, Mike was set for life. He invested in, of all things, a Car Wash business. When mother, Gege died she left Fran very little. Most of the money went to Mike and a couple of "friends" who had been managing her money. Bailey was left with no inheritance. His share was left to his children if he had any, otherwise it went to charity. For years to follow, Fran continued to drink and smoke more and had episodes of true psychosis. She required admission to mental hospitals on occasions. This was very difficult for our son, Bailey because he was the one who had to admit her. Fran married again to a man who seemed to accept and tolerate, her drinking and psychosis. The two of them liked Cats: they bred and raised them, took them to Cat Shows and at one time had over ninety cats in their home.

I was given custody of Bailey when he was four years old. His mother was totally incapable of taking care of him so he lived with me and wife number four, Mary (she renamed herself Shannon) along with Sean and Kelli our two other children.

Sometime in 1976 Fran developed cancer of her breast, had the surgery with radiation and was cured. In early 2000 she was admitted to a psychiatric hospital that was part of a general hospital. At this point her diagnosis was not mental illness but pulmonary disease. She should have been in the general medical ICU. She had inadequate treatment and died.

Chapter Seventeen

Plastic Surgery Training 1960

PRECEPTORSHIP WITH "AL DAVIS"
MEET BILL BIXBY

DR. ALBERT DAVIS was one of the fathers of Plastic Surgery in San Francisco and the political world of the specialty. He had spent several years with Dr. Harold Gilles in London and knew first hand of the work done by Dr. Ralph Millard in publishing the two wonderful volumes that peeked my interest forever in Plastic and Reconstructive Surgery. Dr. E. C. Brown was the young associate in practice with Davis. I developed a love affair with "The City by the Bay." San Francisco was full of characters.

THE CHIEF DR. ALBERT DAVIS

Harry Wainwright was a young criminal attorney who worked with Jake Ehrlick, the famous criminal lawyer and was close friends with Jake Ehrlick, Jr. Wainwright had a little tax problem and escapes to Australia. I invested in a land deal with him in Port McQuary and of course lost it all. This was the first of my real estate fiascoes.

During the preceptorship with Dr. Davis I was paid only four or five hundred a month and there was little or no other income. I contributed what I could for the support of my little son, Bailey. Other than that I could hardly afford to buy a newspaper. At the time my friend, Tony Trabert was doing the world tour playing Poncho Gonzales. He happened to come through San Francisco and we had a visit. In the course of our conversation he asked me if everything was good with me. I replied, "Yeah I'm OK but I'm having a hard time paying my bills." He said, "Hey, I have a little extra money now that I could loan you." I said, "No thanks but I love you for offering." He left the next day to play tennis in the Far East. Within three days I received a check for three thousand dollars from his brother, Mark who was an attorney in Cincinnati. There was a note attached that said I could pay him back any time in the future that I could afford it. I took the money to a stockbroker I happened to know and ask him to buy me shares in Frieden Calculator Company. I then went to the bank and borrowed $2000 on the shares. This little amount of extra money made a big difference in my life at the time. The stock went up and split. After one year I was able to sell the shares for double, pay Tony back with interest and have some left.

Chapter Eighteen

BILL BIXBY

BILL BIXBY

I WAS IN plastic surgery training in San Francisco in 1960 when I first met Bill Bixby. He came to my professor's office (Dr. Al Davies) seeking some improvement in a scar on the right side of his face. He had sustained the injury in an accident some time ago but at this time he was finishing his college work at Cal and planned to do some print ad modeling. Dr. Albert Davis did the scar revision surgery and I assisted. This wasn't much of a surgical challenge but by the time the stitches were removed I got to know the patient well.

When Bix learned that I was from Los Angeles and was married to Fran who had made the movie "Giant" with Liz Taylor, Rock Hudson and Jimmy Dean, he became very interested and announced to me that he planned to go to Hollywood and become a big "movie star." I laughed and thought he was kidding but he was dead serious. He wanted to know if I knew any drama coach that could help him. My wife, Fran worked with a very good teacher by the name of Estelle Harmon. I gave him the name and went on about my training with Professor Davis.

I didn't see Bill for six months. He had been in Los Angeles attending Estelle Harmon's acting class and returned to San Francisco to visit with his mother who was one of the buyers at Imagnin. He came by the office as a follow up on his surgery. The scar revision had worked well and it was difficult to even see it. He was happy and notified me that he was sure he was going to be a movie star.

Bixby was a very handsome young man, bright and had a wonderful sense of humor. He was an only child and had a love-hate relationship with his mother. She was a tough lady who insisted on telling him how to live his life and he let her know he didn't like it. He called her by her first name, "Jane." and they were in a constant conflict.

Bixby's life was one of extreme contrasts full of good and bad. His professional career was more than successful while his personal live was crowded with tragedy. I loved the guy. He was intelligent and one of the most witty and humorous people I knew. We saw each other often and our friendship was one of the joys of my life. We played lots of golf at Bel Air Country Club and he thanked me almost every day for sponsoring his membership in that club. During one round, I wasn't playing very well so on the third hole he pulled a cookie out of his pocket and said, "Here eat this and maybe you will play better." It looked like an ordinary chocolate-chip cookie but I was sure it was more. I wondered how it could make me play better but I ate it quickly. He mentioned that it was better if I had nibbled it slowly. I was naive not to know, coming from Bix that it was an "Alice B. Toklis" cookie. At any rate it sure smoothed out my golf swing. My score was 78 and I had never broken 80 before in my whole golf life. I tried many times in the future to get him to give me another of those cookies but he never would.

Over the years I did several cosmetic surgeries for him. The first was his eyelids. His story was that during the making of a movie he was required to hang on to a wing of an old biplane in flight and the wind was so strong he noted his upper eyelids made flapping noises. After that it was his face-lift, then his nose made a little smaller. Bill was a very willing patient. We knew that he was an addictive personality and I think he was always willing to go to surgery just to get the Demerol. He was grateful for my keeping him looking good and he said that one day he would reveal to the world how I had prolonged his career.

After returning from the Hope Ship, I took over a practice in Inglewood California. By this time Bixby was well entrenched in Hollywood. His first break was to appear on the Joey Bishop Show. He played a character that was a dapper dresser and walked around with a big dog wearing matching clothes.

We kept in touch and we became good friends. He began getting better and more significant role. The next was "My Favorite Martian." then "The Courtship of Eddie's Father." two movies with Elvis Presley and "The Hulk" to mention a few. Along the way he married a beautiful lady, Brenda. Of course she was in show business too. I did a breast enlargement on her before she appeared in a movie about a sheriff who cleaned up a corrupt town with a baseball bat. ("Walking Tall"). This seemed like a very happy marriage at first but they had trouble and separated shortly after their son, Christopher was born. When he was five or six years old Brenda wanted him to experience the mountains and it's snow. On the second day at Big Bear Christopher came down with an upper respiratory infection. Aside from a high fever he had a severe sore throat. She took him to a local medical facility that was very busy and was required to wait an unusual length of time. As they waited it gradually became more difficult for the child to breath. By the time he was seen by a doctor his severe throat swelling had completely closed his airway. In medical terms he had a classical case of Ludwig's Angina. The emergency treatment should have been an immediate tracheotomy or at least the passage of an endotracheal tube if it could have been possible to get one passed the swollen vocal cords. Beautiful little Christopher died in the ER on that winter day. Bixby and Brenda were devastated. This super little boy was the one thing that could possibly have saved their marriage. Bill retreated to a small rented house on the beach of Malibu and never came out of it for three months. He smoked Pot, did coke and drank too much. Brenda had been having a problem romance with an ex football player. They had a racial difference and she was very unhappy about that and the divorce from Bill, so add this to the horrible loss of her son. Life was unbearable for her so she put a gun in her mouth and ended it.

After Brenda, Bix never married again for a very long time. We both lived in Condos in Century City as bachelors. We shared a chef who would cook for each of us at least twice a week and many evenings we would follow the cook and have dinner with each other and our girl friends. There was a time when his "Hulk" show was being shot in Vancouver that he met an attractive young lady by the name of Laura. She worked as a receptionist at the hotel where he stayed. This became a serious romance and he asks her to marry him. The wedding was in Hawaii with very few guests. Of course it was professionally filmed. The video was shown at a big party at Chasens. With huge monitors encircling the private room so all of his friends got to enjoy their beautiful Hawaiian wedding. The speeches that followed were fun. Most of them talked abut how long they had known Bixby so when it came my time I said I had known him so long that I think I delivered him when he was born.

The marriage to Laura worked well for a year or two. She needed something to do so she got a job across the street from Century Park where they lived in Century City. It was a strange type of work. She was in charge of coordinating maintenance at the hotel. Perhaps she had done the same at the hotel in Vancouver where Bix met her.

We had dinner one evening at Mister Chaos in Beverly Hills with Don Rio and his wife. We noted that Bill was depressed and for a good reason. Shortly after we ordered drinks He announced to us, in a low sad voice, "I found out today that I have Cancer of the Prostate." What more tragedy could this poor guy endure? He had several options as to treatment and after learning all I could about the biopsy and the X-ray findings I discussed it with my friend. His Urologist was new but he had used the same general practitioner ever since he came to Los Angeles. Bixby was very loyal: he had the same agent, the same medical doctor, the same barber, and the same plastic surgeon for over 25 years.

The recommendation from his Urologist and his GP was to submit to a radical prostatectomy. Here was a fairly young man in a new marriage and in most cases this radical surgery would severely limit, if not destroy his sexual function. In hopes of a cure radical surgery is definitely indicated but there were other types of treatment such as irradiation with radon seeds or proton therapy, etc. I pleaded with Bill to at least explore these other options. His almost fanatic loyalty and faith in the recommendation of his family doctor prevailed and he had the surgery done at Cedars of Lebanon. The operation went well but not long afterward his X-rays revealed pelvic bone metastasis. This was very serious and was accompanied by severe back pain. He adjusted as well as he could and chose to go on working. His writer friends Don Rio and his wife launched a new TV show about a teenage girl and asked Bixby to direct them. He continued to work and even went to Texas to do a film with Willie Nelson. During the time he was away his and Laura's marital anniversary came up. Bill sent a large bouquet to her at their home in Century City. When he arrived home two days later the flowers were sitting on the entry hall table and there was a note propped against the vase. It said, "Bill I am sorry but I can not live with a sick and dying man. Good bye!" Some wife. More tragedy. He continued to have radiation treatments loosing weight and most of his wonderful looking hair. Being the vain actor he didn't even want his closest friends to see him.

Bixby accepted the invitation of a lady friend to come to her house in Hawaii where he could relax and recuperate. She took wonderful care of him and came to love him in spite of his rapidly failing health. They were married in a very private ceremony and were happy together until Bill died in her arms.

Chapter Nineteen

Hope Ship Statistics

AH-7 USS HOPE

- Comfort class Hospital Ship:

- Displacement: 9,800 tons (full load)

- Length: 418'

- Beam: 60'

- Draft: 24'

- Speed: 15.5 knots (max); 13.5 knots (econ)

- Armament: NONE

- Complement: 516; 400+ patients

- Geared turbine engines; single screw; 4,000 hp

- Built at Consolidated Steel, Wilmington, Calif., and commissioned 15 August 1944

"Project HOPE originated during the 'peaceful coexistence' phase of the Cold War. President Dwight Eisenhower convened a 'People to People' conference at the White House in 1955, believing that international citizen exchanges, particularly in the arts, medicine, business, and agriculture, would promote democracy over communism.

Shortly after the conference, the President suffered a heart attack, and during recovery, he met Washington, D.C., cardiologist, Dr. William B. Walsh. As they became better acquainted, President Eisenhower asked Dr. Walsh to submit a medical project for the People to People Program. In 1958, just months after the Soviets launched Sputnik, the first manmade satellite. Dr. Walsh presented his idea for a different kind of circumnavigating satellite--the S.S. HOPE. His vessel would show the world something at which Americans excelled, medicine.

AH-7 USS HOPE

DR. WILLIAM WALSH

Dr. Walsh recruited some 3,000 volunteers for the eleven voyages. They endured cramped quarters, exhausting schedules, and often were met initially with anti-American protests. Radio Moscow portrayed the ship as a floating branch of American center for chemical and bacteriological warfare at Fort Detrick, Maryland. The work, however, changed minds and won hearts. It also changed the volunteers, as one noted: "To be in a situation where people might die, or live in misery, if you weren't there, is meaningful. I thought the HOPE needed me. Now I think I need the HOPE."

With far-flung business and government connections, Dr. Walsh and his closest supporters pulled together Project HOPE. They secured the transfer of the former Navy hospital ship, U.S.S. Consolation, raised private funds to refit it as the S.S. HOPE, persuaded the pharmaceutical industry to donate medicines, and reached hundreds of volunteer doctors, nurses, and public health workers who wanted to participate. All of these elements came together on September 22, 1960, when the ship left San Francisco, for Indonesia and Vietnam.

William B. Walsh, M.D., Project HOPE visionary founder and leader for 34 years of its 40-year history, later received numerous honors from grateful countries.

After finishing my training period I took a busman's holiday to serve as the first plastic surgeon on this Hospital Ship Hope in south East Asia. The "Hope Ship" was anchored in the harbor of Saigon. (Often referred to as the Paris of the Orient). There was Patients galore, both civilian and military. We received dozens of letters of appeal for treatment by the American doctors. There was no way we could take care of them all so we knew the best we could do was to take a sampling of all the surgical cases and train their doctors so they could carry on after we left.

The military hospital was full of severely wounded and burned patients caused by phosphorus grenades and flamethrowers. Many of the wounded needed skin grafts. Their equipment and supplies were poor or non-existing. At the University Hospital in Saigon we found a Dermatome (for cutting skin grafts) in a box that had never been opened. When asked why they had never used it, the reply was, "We didn't know how to put it together." With a mood of excitement and celebration, this very useful instrument was put to work in order to harvest badly needed skin to resurface the terribly burned patients. Otherwise they were left to heal by scar formation and contracture leaving horrible deformities. When the first days work was finished we celebrated with cocktails of Coca-Cola.

On most visits to the Saigon hospitals we would take our own instruments that we needed. When seeing these delicate tools the local doctors would imply that if they had these specialized instruments they would be able to do the work as well. Of course we wound up giving them the instruments. As a result we decided not to take anything from the ship and make do with what was available in their hospitals. It was difficult but proved to be the best way to prove to them that we were there to teach and help them rather than to show off our superior equipment. I hasten to say that we learned as much from the Vietnam doctors as they did from us, especially in the area of diagnosing and treating tropical diseases. We were shown illnesses and conditions there that we had never seen before or ever read about in textbooks. Mixed infections such as Noma caused by mothers rubbing the teething gums of their children with dirty hands, setting up infections that destroyed all tissue of the cheeks resulting in grotesque deformities. These cases presented a real challenge for reconstruction because they required restoring all three layers of the cheek including skin, muscle and mucosal lining. Under normal circumstances most of these cases would require multiple staged procedures over a three to six week period. We were there for a limited period of time so we did the most we could in one stage. Some of the more serious cases would be transported back to the hospital ship where we had the most modern equipment to work with. The local doctors were always invited to accompany their patients aboard for observation and lectures. We would give them books and journals also until we depleted our library to their bare shelves.

The only Vietnamese plastic surgeon I encountered was a lady who's office and home was in the suburbs of Saigon. Dr. Nguin was the only one there doing cleft lip children. I scrubbed with her on a case and noted that she scrubbed in sterile water. We always scrub our hands in the regular tap water at our sinks. I thought this was interesting. Here in a remote area of the world this lady had better sterile technique than we did and she was a marvelous surgeon.

While in Saigon, on the Hope Ship, my older brother, Bill died in his flower hothouse of a massive heart attack. I returned to be with Virginia, Bill's widow when I learned that a lady was looking for me. She was the wife of a young plastic surgeon who had committed suicide over her wanting a divorce. She wanted to sell me his practice. The doctor was Harold Stein who had developed a very busy practice, covering five emergency rooms from Inglewood to Long Beach. His work was exceptional and his records were perfect. I walked into his well-equipped office and went to work. Our financial deal was that I would agree to pay her one half of my first year's gross earnings with three years to pay it. It was a good deal. She got somewhat over $100,000 and I got a going practice. My payment was considered payment for his equipment, furnishings and remainder of his lease all of which could be depreciated for tax purposes. Goodwill was valuable but this item could not be depreciated.

The office was in Inglewood, California. I bought a small house (509 St. Johns Place) two blocks from Daniel Freeman Hospital. Luckily I inherited a wonderful office manager, Norma who knew every thing about this practice and helped me prepare two volumes of cases to qualify for those board exams. I took and passed the plastic surgery boards in 1964.

At this time I was married to Mary (Shannon) and we had our son Sean, then Kelli four years later. Sean was a perfect big brother. He always aspired to be in show business as a writer-producer, and has demonstrated amazing tenacity over six or more years and has written and produced his own film.

Kelli has become a very successful actress doing a TV show "The Practice" for seven years.

Chapter Twenty

———⋆———

The Surgical Dressing Room

ONE MORNING AS I was changing into my surgical scrubs at the Little Company of Mary Hospital in Torrance, California there were four or five other doctors there, two of whom had finished their surgery and were changing to their street clothes. It was about eleven o'clock in the morning. One of the doctors said, "this is the third time I have changed my clothes this morning at three different hospitals. Who else does this as part of their livelihood? Some times I feel like a "Parisian whore"! Another doctor was describing a tumor that he had just removed from a woman's abdomen, "You can't believe how big this damn tumor was" and he was actually laughing as he said, "it was the size of a small watermelon." Another was talking about a little six-year-old girl that he had in the hospital for some diagnostic tests. She was so precocious that she wore full facial make up and a wig with a spare one hanging on a mold at the bedside. An oriental physician, who had been quietly listening to this description said, "what's she in for a D and C?" (Dilatation and Curettage is the procedure for scraping out the uterus as for an abortion). After a quiet moment of continued dressing, someone mentioned that he thought the human body, even though it is a miracle of design, could have been altered for more convenience. Say for example, the urinary tract could have been brought out your right index finger so when driving along in your car and had to urinate you could just stick your finger out the window and go. Another guy said, "Yeah it would really be convenient if that were true and the vagina had been placed on the upper arm. When a guy saw an interesting woman he could go up to her and, as he punches her shoulder with his index finger say, "haven't I met you somewhere before?"

Chapter Twenty One

Mary Wilcox Wife Four

ONE AFTERNOON AFTER golf at Bet Air Country Club, a new friend from the foursome asked me to have dinner with him at his club. His wife was out of town for the week. He was the owner of the Millionaires Club, members only, that was located at Burton Way and La Cienega. The building looked like a giant spider. There was a very private club within a club in the below-street level called the Cave. After dinner he wanted me to see the Cave. His manager had told him about a new girl he had hired that was special. He said her name was Mary Wilcox and she was fresh in town from Boulder, Colorado. The waitresses in the Cave were also the entertainers. They were dancer/singers and dressed similar to Playboy Bunnies. Mary was special: very attractive and had great legs. She met the owner and served us drinks then she did her number on stage. I was taken with her and my new friend knew it. He informed me that his employees' could not date the members. I informed him that I was not a member. With that he whipped out a card, gave it, to me and said; "Now you are." I came back to the club a few days later to see Mary again. She served me and paid for the drinks herself. I didn't know this until later because I had left enough money on the table to pay the bill with a ten-dollar tip. Mary had been in Los Angeles only a few months and working at this club had been her first job.

She lived in a small apartment in Manhattan Beach. Usually it was two or three in the morning when she finished work. She went to her little car got in, and started to drive out of the parking lot. Suddenly a man popped up out of the back seat, put a knife to her throat and told her to drive to her apartment. He seemed to know about her and that she lived alone in Manhattan Beach. Mary was amazingly clever when she agreed to do what he told her and then after talking to him for a while said, "If it's sex you want, I'm all for it but why don't we stop at this late spot I know and have drink first." The man relaxed, put his knife away and agreed. They went to a place on Santa Monica Boulevard and ordered drinks. She faked having a good time and after the "would be rapist" had two or three drinks and really relaxed she excused herself to go to the toilet. While there she called the police. They came and arrested the guy. She was very shaken by the incident but really kept her "cool." So much for a dumb criminal. She had this jerk believing she really liked him. After I heard that story I knew she definitely had some acting talent and possibly could 'do well in "tinsel town." Little did I know that this acting business would be her obsession?

We dated for about a year and were married in the fall of 1965. The wedding was in Boulder, Colorado, Mary's hometown. Tony Trabert was my best man. This being my fourth marriage, I needed no rehearsal but I was given a serious lecture by the priest on how I should make this marriage last. (Little did he know).

We lived in a sweet little house on St. Johns Place in Inglewood. This was within walking distance of Daniel Freeman a fine Catholic hospital with a very busy emergency room. I had just passed my specialty boards in Plastic Surgery (1964) and was on staff of five hospitals in the area. I was very busy and hardly a day went by that I was not called to treat an emergency in one of those hospitals. The calls were mostly at night and they were usually due to traffic accidents or gun shot wounds.

We were very happy on St. Johns Place. Our son Sean was born at Daniel Freeman Hospital on March 8, 1966.

Mary continued to pursue her acting career in spite of the conflicting demands as wife and motherhood.

WIFE NUMBER FOUR MARY WILCOX (SHANNON)

We moved from St. Johns Place in Inglewood to a house on Beverly Drive in Beverly Hills. By that time I was doing more and more cosmetic surgery and the main source of those patients was from "Tinsel Town". In order to upgrade this change in my practice I opened a second office in Century City. Kelli was born on June 8, 1970 It was around this time that we met Timothy Simms, an interior designer who was to become a tenaciously, integral part of our lives.

Tim Sims came along at the right time to help Shannon with the new house. He not only became our "live in decorator." he wanted to take over the full management of our lives. When someone is willing to do this and it appeared he knew what he was doing, the temptation was to let him do it. As a result one day you find out that you have given up too much control and he had to go. Tim was very good at almost everything.

Life on Beverly Drive was good. The house was beautiful, but there was no pool and no tennis court. It did have wonderful sidewalks.

Refuge from a marriage that could not compete with a career obsession. The attempt to move to Palm Springs with a new office at One Hawkeye Park, decorated by Steve Chase and Snuffie Adams. I bought the Condo at The Springs Country club in Rancho Mirage. Shannon would not consider moving away from Hollywood (seems I heard this before from another wife, Fran). The condo was kept for five years, as was the lease on the office.

A visit from Shannon that was only the second in all the time I had the place. A surprise visit in which I am sure she thought she would catch me with another woman but it didn't work. However, it was that evening she informed me she wanted a divorce so she could pursue her career more aggressively.

The divorce of course came with its emotional and financial trauma. I sold the Bel Air home and giving all the money to the woman who actually attended a night class at UCLA to learn how to get the most our of a divorce. She learned well! However in California the man doesn't have a chance. He pays forever unless he is an unemployed bum. The marriage lasted nineteen years and for the first ten years it was a very happy time. Lots of great memories but as the years rolled by and her career never caught on. Shannon seemed to be shrouded in a mood of desperation. When she would go out on interviews for a role she would overact and lose the job.

The divorce settlement: all the cash, a small home in Brentwood, free and clear of debt and mortgage, and six thousand a month for life or until she remarried, either of us died or further order of the court plus one half of the Pension and Profit funds, as of 1984.

Shannon hired a ruthless attorney who talked her in to suing me and several other people around me including her stepson, Bailey. By this time Bailey had created a tech company that looked very good and he had a tech stock portfolio worth around 6.5 million dollars.

Of course Bailey was hurt that the woman that had been his mother since he was four years old would sue him. He managed not to let them know his net worth and when it came to settlement I needed a loan of over $250,000 to pay her. It was a short-term loan until I could sell some of my Inamed stock. Bailey could have easily loaned me the money but he wouldn't for fear they would come after him for more money. I had to get the loan from Dick Babbitt.

It has been over ten years and Bailey has not fully recovered nor stopped hating Shannon. He hardly communicates with any of the family including me and says he doesn't need nor want any family. He says that being family oriented is not who he is. He lives totally alone yet has had several wonderful women that he might have married and created his own family that he surely could have cared about. Ironically when his grand mother died she left a large amount of money to his mother, Fran, skipped Bailey and left his share to Bailey's children. If he has no children it will go to charity.

As mentioned earlier in this book there is what I believe to be a genetic defect in his mother's family that allows them to ignore clutter. They don't see clutter and don't care. Dirty clothes are piled on the floor in the corner of a closet, dirty dishes are left all over the kitchen, loose money change is scattered on the bed room floor, the bed is not made and the bathroom is filthy. At the risk of being cruel and critical I have tried to talk to him about this and to gently inform him that I think this is the main reason he has not been able to attract a woman that he might want to marry. There was one really spectacular lady that I think really cared about him. After spending some time with him in his home she said good-bye. This really hurt him because he was truly in love with her. He wouldn't accept this as being important and refused to do anything about it.

After six marriages I can assure him that I know most women cannot and will not live in his environment for long no matter how much they love him. His mother, Fran was the only one out of my six ex-wives that had this genetic defect. (His grandmother Bailey was the worst.) He has it.

After our long conversation by phone on July 4, 2007 I expressed my concern about our family not caring about each other enough to keep in touch and seeing each other as often as we could. I take full blame for choosing the wrong mothers. My children were not taught the value of togetherness and especially the value of LOVE. Three of them (Eva Gabor, Fran Benedum, and Shannon Wilcox) were more obsessed and in love with their movie careers than with anything else.

I sensed from our conversation that Bailey is not happy and has not been for the past ten years. He claims that this non-caring person is "who he is". He doesn't think he needs family, only a couple of friends. The only thing he really needs is someone to love him.

Chapter Twenty Two

Friends The Scotts

M.B. SCOTT, ONE of the most outrageous people I ever knew, his wife at the time, Nini, and my wife at the time, Mary (later renamed herself Shannon) took a trip to Europe together in the summer of 1980. This vacation was one of the great memories of my life. We had argued over who would get the limo for our shuttle to the airport and M.B, insisted. We were to leave around nine AM in order to catch our 8:15 flight. Mary and I were packed and ready. It was getting close to

MB SCOTT & WIFE NINI

nine and they had not arrived. We became concerned and called their house to learn that they had just left. At nine fifteen the limo pulled up to our house. Nini had a large hat pulled down almost over her eyes, she was crying and held a makeup sponge under her nose to catch the nasal routed tears. M.B. was cheerful as though nothing was wrong. As we got seated in the car he asked Nini if she had his cigarettes. She replied, "Get your own damn cigarettes." Of course we asked why she was crying. The story was that at breakfast he had asked for some ketchup for his scrambled eggs. She gave him a fresh bottle that happened to be an off brand type. As he took the bottle and looked at it he said, "this is not Heinz, it's an inferior brand. I don't eat anything but the best." With that he emptied the whole bottle on the floor. This was the beginning of our three weeks together. We arrived to the ramp as the plane was just pulling away. M.B went to the ramp window, caught the captain's eye and with his hands in the praying position and in pantomime begged him to return for us and he did. I had never heard of an airliner moving away to have ever returned for a late passenger. Things like that seem to always happen to M.B. No matter where we shopped and found Mr. Scott missing we could always find him in the nearest jewelry stores buying something for himself. One of our stops was the Calla de Volpe Hotel on the Island of Sardinia. It happened to be M.B's birthday and we were at a loss as to what kind of gift we could come up with to give him at the dinner that evening. We knew he had already purchased a suitcase full of goodies for himself so we decided to sneak all of his recent purchases from his luggage, wrap all twenty or more of them and place them in the center of the table. This hotel had a fabulous dinning room filled with elegant people. Our table was in the center of the room. As we toasted him and he began unwrapping the packages, he soon realized what we had done, yet he played the room like a great actor, loudly extolling our magnificent taste in the choice of the birthday gifts we had so generously selected for him.

When we arrived in Athens M.B. and I both had run out of pocket money so we went to the nearest American Express office. He put down his green card and the teller said she could give him only four hundred dollars on his card. He was disgruntled and muttered something about that wasn't enough even for tipping purposes. American Express had just shortly before the time of our trip came out with the gold then later the platinum cards. I laid down my gold card and the lady said, "How much do you want." My friend was embarrassed when I got a thousand dollars. It was rare that one could zing Scott so I couldn't resist. I said, "M.B. If I had known you had only the green card I would not have come on this trip with you"

Another time M.B. wanted Nini to take his picture while he was sitting, muscles flexed, on the wall at Rhodes. She had trouble with the camera so he said, "John, take the camera, for Christ sake, she has the mind of a white rat" The fight was on again.

The cruise ship we took through the Greek Islands made a brief stop at Effaces in Turkey. After visiting the ruins we did some shopping at a beach side bizarre. M.B. thought he had found the perfect gifts for Christmas. They were the shoes with curled up toes, alabaster eggs and other cheap Turkish stuff. He was so happy with his purchases that he wanted to thank the merchant in Turkish. Mary had been our interpreter in most of the countries we visited so M.B. asked her how to say "thank you in Turkish." It was another great moment to zing Scott, which he deserved. She said, "M.B. I thought everybody knew How to say thank you in Turkish" He said, "Well what is it." She said, "gobble, gobble."

I purchased a larger home in Bel Air on St. Cloud. Mary (Shannon) was angered by the fact that I purchased the home without her approval and she never took much interest in making this fabulous house into a home. Her obsession with her career dominated her life.

In old Bel Air there were many prominent neighbors: Sonny Bono, Johnny Carson, Larry Flynt, and Kenny Rogers.

It was a great joy and privilege to belong to the Bel Air Country Club. I joined the club in 1964 and had the honor to serve on the board of directors for three years. Golf is a great game and gives the members the opportunity to meet and get to know some fascinating people. It is such a friendly club that you could always get a game and sometimes it would be with a person that was very well known that you probably couldn't get an appointment with them off the course if you tried. Yet with golf you had the opportunity to spend four hours with them. It became the center of our social life.

BELAIR HOME ON ST. CLOUD

Tim Sims gave us one party when we moved into the Bel Air home. It was sensational. Andy Williams said it was the best party he had ever been invited to. He had the ability to make you feel that you could not live without him. Two weeks after I let him go he was driving up LaCienega to Hollywood Boulevard, stopped at intersection and two Hispanics jumped out of some bushes, opened the passenger side door and at gun point demanded money. Timothy challenged them and was killed by a shot to his head.

SEAN

KELLY

BAILEY WITH SWEETS

We had a wonderful white Samoyed dog named Sweets who roamed
the yard supposedly for security but he was so sweet, as his name

implied that if an intruder came into the grounds he would prob-ably welcome him and lick his hands. One of the neighbors gave our children a pigmy goat that quickly became great friends with Sweets. They played together and chased each other, usually Sweets chasing the goat. The yard was multilevel and occasionally the goat would sud-denly jump to a higher level and the dog could not figure out where he went. It was great fun to watch them, this strange friendship. The goat turned out to be pregnant, not by Sweets, the dog, which would have been very interesting.

THE PREGNANT PIGMY GOAT

She was impregnated before we got her by a normal sized goat. When it came time for the delivery, it was my job as the doctor to become suddenly a goat obstetrician. I was up all night attending this birth without success. The kid was just too large to pass through the small pelvis of the pigmy mother. I was scheduled to do surgery that morning so I called my brother, Jim, to come take the poor goat to the vet. He came with my secretary, Joan, and our head nurse, Patty. Both of who seemed more concerned about this poor animal in great labor pains than they were about our human patients. They put the goat in the front seat of Dr. Jim's Rolls Royce and headed over to the San Fernando Valley to a vet we knew by the name of Dr. Puttnie. The goat was making loud goat noised because of the pain and these two ladies were doing their best to comfort her. Joan was holding the animal in her lap and Patty leading over from the back seat with her butt in the air, trying to help. I have often wondered what they would have said to a policeman had they been stopped for speeding, which they were. Putney, the vet did a cesarean operation and delivered a stillborn kid.

Chapter Twenty Three

Kelli

RAY BOGER AND KELLY WILLIAMS
(STRAW MAN FROM WIZARD OF OZ)

KELLI WILLIAMS (MY only daughter) was born prematurely at Daniel Freeman Hospital in Inglewood, California on June 8, 1970. She weighed only 4 lbs.

If anyone described a perfect child she would be the model. She came through the medical problems of being born early with no complications. (Little girl preemies are known to handle this problem better than little boys). She was beautiful, smart and a joy. Of course being my only daughter made her very special. Kelli made excellent grades at Beverly Hills High School and was very active in their drama program. She did the senior plays so well that after graduation two women agents told her they thought she was talented enough that she could work as an actress. They offered to represent her. She asked me what I thought. Whether she should go on to college or try show business. I told her I could see no harm in giving the agents a try. If it didn't work she could go on to college. Kelli made over $100,000 her first year and has worked ever since. She did a series: "The Practice" for seven years. Which was about a law firm. Then for a year "Medical Investigation" among other jobs. During this time she was married and now has three beautiful children. She has always had her priorities healthy. Her family and marriage come first unlike her mother, Shannon who always let it be known that her acting career took precedence over every thing else in her life.

Mary Shannon met a man on the chair lift in Aspen, Colorado. He mentioned that he was a tennis instructor (pro) and lived in Los Angeles and that he was available for private lessons. At the time we lived in Bel Air, an upscale residential area in west Los Angeles. We had our own pool and tennis court. Shannon mentioned our address and the pro said that he knew the property because he had given lessons to the former owners, the McCullocks. Interesting coincidence. She was impressed and arranged for him to schedule some lessons for our family. He would not give her his real name and address and insisted that he would contact her. He told her to just call him "Ed."

We should have been suspicious of this man's character and motives when he preferred to remain anonymous. At the time Kelli was around three years old. Which would be 1973. She was yet too young for lessons but the rest of our family took weekly instructions. Sean was only five. Bailey was the oldest child living with us at the time. "Ed" became a prominent figure in our lives. For the next seven years and in all this time we never knew his real name. He continued to call us to schedule more lessons over time, and during these phone conversations he preferred not to call me by my name and assigned me the nickname "R.J." When I insisted on knowing his full real name and address or at least a phone number he explained that he was a poor student and wanted to be paid in cash in order to avoid income tax.

Ed was a good teacher and was always curious about my Plastic Surgery practice and me. During the process of picking up the tennis balls there was always many questions about my work such as anatomy and operative procedures. Because of his ever presence we became comfortable with him always being around.

As the years went by Ed gradually developed a "Charles Manson" type mind control over Shannon. I was very busy in my practice earning the money to afford our life style. I had no idea what was going on behind my back. By the time Kelli was eight years old Ed had taken over Shannon and Kelli's lives. He considered himself a better teacher than the schools and convinced Shannon to take Kelli out of school and let him tutor her in the library at UCLA. He did this for a full year or longer, stood over her and would not let her even look up from her work for hours at a time. By 1983 Ed had convinced Shannon to divorce me and had her enroll in a class at UCLA on "how to get the most out of a divorce." She learned very well and was convinced that she would do much better in advancing her acting career if she was single. She always admitted to me that her career was more important than the home, children or our marriage.

Sometime around 1982 Shannon got to do a film in El Paso with Jack Nickelson and would be away from home for four months. Without my knowledge or consent she arranged for Sean, age nine, to spend a full school year with his uncle, Bob, in Saudi Arabia and sent Kelli to live in Connecticut with some people we hardly knew.

Over the years things of value would disappear from our home such as jewelry, cuff links and two guns that were given to me by my lawyer. This became so common we had a new alarm system installed. The robberies continued. The only one that had complete access to our home was Ed.

Some time later I learned that he had sustained a head injury during a fight in a bar. He was struck in the head with a bear bottle and became mentally impaired. Attempts to find him since that time have failed.

Kelli is now happily marriage to a good man and they have three beautiful children.

KERIN, SARAME, AND RAVI

Chapter Twenty Four

Aesthetica

IN 1986 WE moved our offices from the seventh floor in Century City to Aesthetica at 5757 Wilshire Blvd. This was an eleven thousand square foot, freestanding surgery center in the mid Wilshire district of Los Angeles. It was designed by Snuffie Adams. There were three fully equipped operating rooms, a ten-bed recovery room, five exam rooms, and a conference room that could seat sixty people. There was closed circuit television from the OR to our conference room. This was a first class facility, licensed and Medicare Certified with nineteen employees. The facility was on the ground floor at the back of what used to be Aurbachs Department store. There was a Carriage Trade Driveway that was perfect for the privacy of our patients. My secretary and office manager was Joan Chatterton. She was a fantastic lady and knew more about me than I did.

By this time brother Jim and I were beginning to show our age so we did face lifts on each other. We used to be identical twins until we did the surgery and now you can see which one is the best surgeon.

Our first associate member of our staff was Garth Fisher. He had just finished his training. Garth's father was sent to Korea and never came back. I was so fond of him that I felt like his surrogate father.

Dr. Fisher worked with us for over eight years then moved his practice to Beverly Hills. He became famous when he did the TV show "Extreme Makeover" for ABC.

Our lease was for ten years and we had a very happy practice there. Sometime in 1994 Dr Jim and I decided it was time for us to sample some of our own services so we did face-lifts on each other. Before the surgery we were identical twin. After you could tell who was the best surgeon.

DR. GARTH FISHER AND ME

When the lease was up in 1996 we chose not to renew. This was when the economy was bad and real-estate values poor.

After closing our big surgicenter, Aesthetica, Jim and Lavenia moved back to her hometown of Cookeville, Tennessee and I took a small office on Bedford St.in Beverly Hill. I shared the office with Dr. Eugene Worton.

Don McGhan appointed me to the board of directors of Inamed Corporation on December 15, 1996. I continued to work for a couple of years, sharing my time between Beverly Hill, Palm Springs and the corporate offices in Santa Barbara.

Aesthetica entrance

Aesthetica Reception

DR. JOHN'S OFFICE AT AESTHETICA

DR JIM'S OFFICE AT AESTHETICA

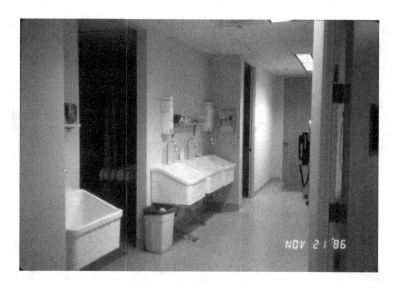

SCRUB AREA AT AESTHETICA

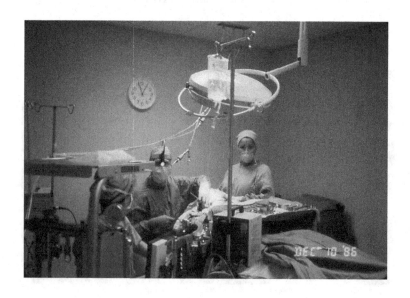

OPERATING ROOM AT AESTHETICA

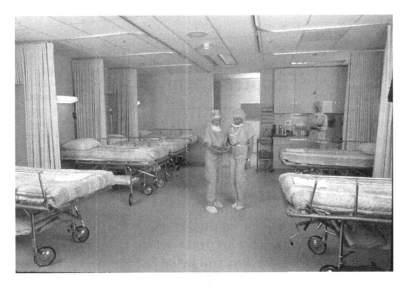

RECOVERY ROOM AT AESTHETICA

CONFERENCE ROOM AT AESTHETICA

Chapter Twenty Five

Brother Jim

DR JIM HAD a propensity for unusual events in his life. Here are two such experiences described in his own words:

"In early 1992, while we were still living in Los Angeles, California, I was driving a four door Jaguar that was burgundy in color. I drove into my garage, having arrived home from my office, about seven o'clock in the evening. My coat was in the back seat on the left side of the car. As I was retrieving it in preparation for going into the house, I was suddenly distracted by something behind me. On turning around, I found myself looking down the barrel of a large handgun. The assailant was a young man wearing a ski mask and a pair of dark woolen gloves. He was shaking badly and was obviously scared as much as I was. I tried to buy some time by talking to him to see just what was going down. By this time I had moved toward the front of my car near the door that led from the garage into our service porch. At this time he had the gun right against my head, demanding my money.

I am a stubborn Texan and I was not about to give in to his demands without some sort of resistance. From the corner of my vision, I happened to see a small pipewrench laying on the corner of the chest that was in front of my car. He said again, "give me yo money man, I is gona blow yo head off"'.

It was about this time that he noticed my wrist watch and I am sure that he thought that it was an expensive Rolex, it was not a Rolex I said to him "you want my watch - take it - go ahead take it off'. At the same time, as a means of distraction, I was shaking my wrist in front of his face. He had an accomplice waiting out side and I was afraid if I let him in the house they would possibly rape my wife and then loot our home. This is exactly why I did not want him to get into our home. I knew that he would, while holding us at gunpoint, signal his partner from the window to come in and help him. What had happened to some friends of ours not too long before, and the incident was still fresh in my mind I continued to shake my wrist watch in front of his face and at the same tome I reached for the pipe wrench with my right hand. My plan was to strike him on the left side of his head with the wrench. He was quick and raised his left shoulder to ward off my blow. My wrenches hit him on the shoulder, then on the left side of his head. At the same time that I hit him with the wrenches he drew his pistol back and struck me on the head just behind the left ear. I was fortunate because he could have squeezed the trigger faster than he had drawn the gun back to strike me. Blood from the wound that he had inflicted started squirted out all over everything. I must have raddled him because he turned and ran out of the garage. I expected any second for him to turn and let me have one or two shots. To make myself less of a target, I ducked down in front of my car. Believe me the burgundy color of my car took on a brighter red color as I continued to bleed profusely from the wound. Fortunately I did not loose consciousness and was thus able to stay behind the car. I was sure that I had been shot. , As an old duck hunter, I had fired many shots from my 12 gauge, none of them seemed as loud as his blow to my skull when he hit me with the gun. Later the police looked carefully for a bullet that might be lodged somewhere close by - they couldn't find anything.

I waited long enough for my assailant to leave and then I came out from behind the car and immediately closed the garage door with the automatic switch on the wall. I still had the wrenches in my right hand and used them to knock on the back door to alert my wife. I say wrenches because it was not until I activated the garage door switch that I realized that I had picked up a crescent wrench along with the pipe wrench. I actually had two wrenches instead of one.

My wife, Lavenia, came to the back door when she heard all of the knocking and shouted at me through the door to find out who was making all of the noise. I told her it was me and to quickly open the door. I had been shot. When she first saw me standing at the door, all covered with blood, it was quite a shock to her. I reassured her that I was all right, but I needed some medical attention.

I asked her to call the police at 911 and to tell them to send the paramedics too. The first to arrive was the fire department. My wife would not let them in at first until she could see them from the window. She was afraid that my assailant had returned. It did not help that the person that she saw trying to get in had no uniform on. At that time she glanced in the direction of the street and saw his vehicle, it was a fire truck. When she finally let him in one of the first things that he asked her was "where is the victim"? She said, "He is back sitting on the toilet". What she meant was, that I didn't wanting to get blood all over the house. I had closed the lid on the toilet in the maids quarters, which was immediately off of the service porch and it had a linoleum floor covering. I had elected to sit down there while applying pressure to the wound.

The paramedics arrived in no time and after applying a pressure dressing to my head, took me up the hill to Mulholland Drive and their first aid station where they had a helicopter waiting. After transferring me to another stretcher and then into the waiting helicopter, they proceeded to take me directly to the Northridge Trauma Center down the hill in the San Fernando Valley. I had for many years wanted someday to see the valley from the air, but from my present viewpoint all I could see was the ceiling of the helicopter.

Only after they had X-rayed my skull was I able to see and to admit that the noise from the blow was created by his gun striking my head and not from a bullet. The doctor on duty at the E.R. shaved my hair around the wound and proceeded to clean it up. He first tied off the artery that was causing all of the bleeding and then proceeded to do a nice job in sewing me up. He then released me to the care of my brother, who had arrived there sometime earlier, and to my wife.

I was relating all of this one day to a friend of mine who was also a fellow member of the board of directors for the Bell Air country club. Art listened to me intently and then he said, "Jim, I admire your guts, but I am not sure that it was too smart". It was only a short time later that the wife of another friend of ours from the club had returned home from the grocery store. It was about 10:30 A.M. and as she too was getting out of her car there in the driveway 'of her home, she was attacked by a young man with a knife. He stabbed her several times, took all of her jewelry and her money and fled down the hill.

All of this was very unsettling to me and to my wife. We soon decided to leave the area and to go back to Tennessee, Lavenia's home state, to be close to her family and to care for her elderly mother".

In August of 1994, we moved into a new house in Cookeville. It was new to us. The former owner had elevated the back yard some ten or twelve feet before putting in a very nice swimming pool. He had also spent considerable money in dredging out the 16-acre lake that is accompanying our home. We had purchased the north end of the lake as a part of our property. I love to fish and began right away to look for a small boat that would fit our needs. We finally found one and had it tied up on the north bank of the lake. We had recently put a new fence around our pool and the back yard with automatic gate to keep our big red dog in. He had always been inside a fenced area and was not "street smart". On this day I had driven through the gate and closed it. I needed to retrieve something from the boat. It had been raining and the grass on the way down to the boat was wet. I was wearing tennis shoes at the time and of course they were wet when I got back to the car. After checking on the dog and thinking he was inside, I got into the car and at the same time hit the remote control to open the gate. I had not buckled my seat belt yet as I started to back around. My wife thought I was gone so she let "Jimbeau" our dog out the back door to do his thing. She did not realize that I had delayed my trip by going first down to the boat. I glanced to the right just in time to see "Jimbeau" come around the corner of the garage. I had already activated the gate opener and could not stop it in the middle of its cycle. I guess that I panicked for I did not want him to get out of the back yard. I tried to divert his attention by calling him as I opened the left front door of the car. At the same time I slammed on the brake in an attempt to stop. My wet tennis shoe slipped off of the brake on to the accelerator and became jammed between the brake and the gas pedal. The car shot back of course and I desperately tried to hold on to the steering wheel with my right hand. The centrifugal force was too much however and I started to go out the door. At the same time I was still holding on. It is a good thing that I did because I was unknowingly turning the car away from a brick wall and a row of large trees. The car dragged me across the cement drive way on to the grass before I finally lost my grip. The left front wheel then ran over my leg as the back of the car was heading for the swimming pool. It is a good thing the pool was uphill otherwise the station wagon would have ended up in the swimming pool. As it was, after I had been thrown from the car, it went about one half way up the hill before it stopped on its own. I limped over to the car and closed the gate with the remote control. I then called the house on my car phone. The first thing that I asked about was whether "Jimbeau" was in the house and, my wife, Lavenia assured me that he was there in the house with her. It seems that with all of the commotion he had run back to the house for safety.

I told her I had had a little mishap and would she meet me at the front door with her mothers' walker. I was able to drive the car through the automatic gate and around to the front. Lavenia could hardly believe her eyes when she first saw me. My clothing was in shreds and I was bleeding from several wounds and I could only walk on the walker. After her initial shock she took me into the bathroom and tried to clean me up. I changed my clothing and she took me to the hospital for X-Rays. It was at that time that I realized how lucky I had been. Thanks to the soft grass and ground the X-Rays showed that my fibula, the small bone in the lower leg was the only fracture that I had. It was broken in two places. The tibia or weight bearing longer and larger of the two bones was intact. Well, I healed in no time as I wore a special splint on my left leg and foot." This is a story for Ripley about a guy who ran over his own leg with a car he was driving.

Chapter Twenty Six

Tish Martinson
Wife Number Five

Tish Martinson

TISH WAS BORN on the island of St. Maartin in the Caribbean that was half-Dutch and half-French. Her father's families were the merchants and controlled the shipping and commerce. They built the desalination plant that furnished fresh water to the population. Her mother's family was more native French. They came from a fairly long line of settlers and controlled a major part of the real estate on the French side of the island. The two families had conflicting interests and for years had been feuding over control, and literally hated each other. Tish's mother and father were teenagers when they meet and had an affair. Like most teenagers they did not care much about major family interests at the time. Their hormones were in control. The families did not approve of the relationship and weren't about to condone a marriage between the two even after it became know that her mother was pregnant. The child was born out of wedlock, both families were devout catholic, and never acknowledged the existence of this beautiful baby girl. She was furnished a small home with a nanny, full time, paid for all her expenses but would not admit she existed. Here was a child that was being raised totally without parental love. The nanny, unfortunately, was not a good surrogate mother. She treated the situation as a job rather than an adoption and was strict and non-caring. The nanny would take Tish to church on Sundays. She would set in the back, middle of the pews, her mother's family on one side and the father's family on the other, neither would acknowledge the child's presence. Fortunately she was enrolled in the catholic school on the Dutch side where she found not only education but also much needed caring and nurturing. The nuns and Jesuit priests became her family. She was not only a beautiful girl child but she was extremely intelligent and talented. One other saving grace was that she fell in love with the nature of the island. She would spend every moment she could outside at the beach or enjoying the garden aspects of the tropical paradise. She learned not only the names of all the ocean creatures, which became her friends, but all the plant life as well. As she grew into her teen years and became more beautiful and precocious, the men of this small island world began to notice her lustfully. Her story was well known among the community and she became the target of sexual interest to some of the older men on the island, one of whom was a Protestant minister. She was considered the "bad seed." an evil bastard child born out of wedlock and sent there to tempt the men with her sexual beauty. Thanks again to the Nuns and Priests of the catholic school she had some protection. Yet even the Priests were suspected of having lustful intent with this woman/child. Aside from the church she lead a lonely life. The little house in which she lived with the Nanny was in the country where she could ride her small horse that had been given to her by her maternal grandmother. This grandmother was the only one of the large families that did sneak some visits with Tish. When she was seven years old she wanted to have a birthday party. The Nanny planned it with balloons and all the other favors and food. A list of children was invited and no one came. When Tish was around fifteen years old she could easily pass for age twenty or twenty-one. An American actor came to the island and meet her. His name was Gardner McKay. He had starred in a television series in which he ran a sail boat charter service in the South Pacific. A tall handsome man, who was thirty-five years old at the time, fell in love or at least lusted for this child and she for sure fell in love with him. They saw each other several times during his visit and before he left they went to a little church by themselves and repeated vows of matrimony, promising that they henceforth belonged to each other. This was the only thing they could do since she was definitely under age. The plan was that if she could secure a passport and get off the island she was to meet him on a specific date in Paris at the Maurice Hotel. She was an unloved child, now having met the first love of her life. He promises her they will marry when she comes to him. She manages to get a passport, sells her horse, and flies to Paris to meet her love. When she arrived at the hotel she found out that he had checked out and left no forwarding address. She had little or no money, alone in Paris and not knowing what to do, she sat in the lobby for hours thinking about her options. There was no round trip ticket and no money for a room. A young woman noticed her florin look, came over and asked if she was all right. They talked and she explained her situation. The young lady asked her if she knew how to dance. She answered yes. The lady was one of the dancers in the famous Lido de Paris night cub shows. She put Tish up for the night, took her to the club the next day and got her a job as an apprentice dancer with the company. She became a regular on the show and went on to become one of the top models in Paris. She became a runway model for Yves Saint Laurent and Channel. It was at this time that Paul Louis Welare, one of the wealthiest men in Europe, discovered her. He started Air France and many other enterprises. At the time he was in his early seventies and Tish was not yet twenty-one. They became great friends and he allowed her to live in one of his many homes. At one time as a present he gave her two young cheetahs that she raised and lived with for several years. During these years she never stopped loving and waiting for Gardner McKay to come back and keep his promise made in the little church in St. Martin. When she became famous with her modeling, he found her and would come back into her life from time to time, then leave again. Because of her commitment to him she was never available to other relationship potentials. There were many. She waited for nearly twenty years and finally after having his daughter, Tamara, he promised that if she came to Los Angeles they would be married. She paid for furnishing a home with him and lived with him until the day she came home and found him with another woman. After this and all those years of being available she finally realized her first love was hopeless and over. Tish went on to marry some wealthy, eccentric industrialist back east and had a son, Tareck, by him. He abandoned her and took the two children away and hid them from her. She called upon her old friend Paul Louis who hired a detective to find the children and chartered a plane to bring them back. The next event in Tish's life was her marriage to John Martinson, a very handsome, bright and well-educated businessman. By this time Tish had accumulated a fair amount of money from her modeling career. She used most of her savings to help Martinson establish an oil company. In the early days of their marriage they lived in a rented house on Beverly Drive in Beverly Hills. I lived across the street one block north but did not know them. Martinson came to my office to have his eyes done. I was not available for some reason, so he had the surgery done by my twin brother, Jim (Small World). A terrible, senseless tragedy occurred at that time. It was a warm summer day; painters were working outside near an open window on the second floor. This was the nursery of their six-month-old son, Jarret, who was asleep in his crib. The painters stopped to have their lunch on the scaffolding and one of the plastic bags from their lunch blew into the baby's crib. When he awoke and found the plastic he must have thought it was some kind of toy or a hat. He pulled it over his head. When Tish came to his crib, he was dead from suffocation.

They did very well in the oil business with fancy offices in Houston, Texas, their own Lear Jet and not one but two houses next to each other in Bel Air on Stone Canyon, only two blocks from the famous Bel Air Hotel. They gave lavish parties and got to know everyone who was important at the time including O.J. Simpson, et al. Tish's life couldn't be better. She had another son by Martinson named Erick, a beautiful boy who was born with a congenital ear deformity that impaired his hearing. The good life continued until Martinson made some kind of a huge gamble in an oil deal with an Arab group in South America (Kadaffi country) and overnight lost everything. They had been separated for a while before the business crashed, long enough for her to have another boy child, Torgen by and Italian sculptor. When Martinson took off he had sold everything and left her without even a decent car. I don't think she ever knew what happened and probably doesn't to this day. She is street smart and definitely a survivor, so she managed. There must be more to the story of abandonment and bankruptcy of a $25,000,000 company over night. Martinson moved to Sun Valley, Idaho where he has lived ever since and claims to have nothing, though he apparently lives very well.

I met Tish at the Bel Air Country Club when Torgen was four years old. I had just gone through a divorce in 1984 from Shannon/Mary Wilcox who wanted to be free of marital obligations so she could pursue her acting career unencumbered. I had bought a townhouse on Roscomare Road, high above Bel Air and I had a condominium at the Springs Country Club in Rancho Mirage where I had a second office. Tish lived in a house she had bought in partnership with Kasangian, a jeweler and her long time friend Madelyn Jones. It was a strange partnership in which she did the improvement and decorating, and was allowed to live there until the house sold at which time the profits were to be divided. This was a deal that was definitely structured in her favor. Why would she ever want to sell the property as long as she got the use of the home rent-free? This was a pattern that would be repeated at a later date with me, and prove to be my financial ruin. We dated for a year and mainly due to her poor financial condition she was looking to get married again. I was not. After four failures I was definitely on hold. Even after Shane was born, I was still reluctant to venture into matrimony again.

SHANE AT EIGHT   ARMY – NAVY ACADEMY AGE 16

Shane was born at Cedars of Lebanon with some difficulty, on February 23, l987. He was quite cyanotic and was not resuscitated quickly enough. This could have resulted in his having some cerebral changes that may have caused him to have difficulty with his cognitive skills. To my satisfaction he was never confirmed as having "Attention Deficit Disorder." At any rate he is a very intelligent and beautiful young man. All things considered I decided to go ahead and marry Tish as the right thing to do (my mother again). We had a lovely private wedding ceremony at the Bel Air Hotel. I sold the town house and really stretched financially to buy a beautiful home in the Pacific Palisades. Tish did a great job decorating the home but it was very expensive, as was her pattern in every phase of our new life together.

She loved flowers and some months the floral bill would be four or five thousand dollars.

I once give her a signed blank check for the cleaners. She made it out for $1500, cashed it and never mentioned it. One time she made a trip to Paris to see her old friend Paul Louis with the hopes of convincing him to sell his prize diamond to the Sultan Of Brunei for $100,000,000. Paul Louis was close to 100 years old by this time. He refused to sell his treasure for whatever reason so she returned after two weeks. I had given her plenty of cash for the trip and to be sure she didn't need more I gave her a Platinum American Express Card. When I got the bill at the end of the month I saw that she had charged over $10,000 to my card. When I asked her about this she said, "Oh I meant to tell you, I needed some things." Of course I said, "what things?" She replied that she had purchased quite a few items at Gucci but took them back for a refund of the money. "So where is the money?" She said she spent it. Never mentioned it again or explained it further.

Somehow she had this compulsive need for cash and expensive things. When we had been married for only about nine months, I realized that I had a lot of furnishings and personal items in storage which I wanted to either give to my children or my ex wife, Shannon. When Tish learned that I was to meet them at the storage place for this rather mundane chore, she went ballistic. Screamed at me claiming that I was having a rendezvous with my ex wife and threatened to hit me over the head with a large telephone base. I pushed her and the telephone away from me. She faked injury and claimed that I hit her. She ran to the phone and called the police, screaming to them that I was beating her. They came, made out a report and since they could not find any evidence of her injuries they did not take me to jail. I had never seen this pattern of behavior in her before. It was a rage that came from what I believe to arise from her unloved childhood. She was so insecure that she could not tolerate anyone remotely violating her world. If we were at dinner in a restaurant and I even glanced at another woman anywhere she would react with more rage. It was pathologic. My children were not wanted in our home yet I treated her children with love and respect. One day my daughter, Kelli developed abdominal pain so she called me and I went to my ex wife's home where Kelli lived to examine her for fear she might be developing appendicitis. It was toward the end of the day so I decided to stay there for the night so I could be available if she needed me. I called home and left word on our answering machine as to what I was doing. I slept in my son, Sean's room. The next morning I checked Kelli's abdomen I felt that it was just a painful menstrual ovulation and thought she would be all right. When I pulled away in my car to go to my office I noted a Jag that had backed into a driveway about one half block down the street. As I drove past I realized it was Tish. She pulled out behind me and started ramming into the back of my car. I pulled over and got out to see what in the world she was ramming me for. She then drove toward me trying to run me down and chased me all the way up onto someone's lawn. I have rarely seen such vicious anger in anyone. She then drove away without speaking to me. That evening when I returned home to the Palisades house she had placed all of my clothes into garbage bags and had them out side the front door and I was no longer allowed to enter my own home. Tish was convinced that I had spent the night with my ex wife and paid no attention to my explanation as to why I had been there for the night. Finally I saw no hope for this marriage of only ten months. I was served with divorce papers and was not allowed to come within a hundred yards of the house by restraining order. She had sworn that I had struck her and abused her physically. I could not see my child for over a year and it took me that long to get her out of my house, which was my sole and separate property.

I listed the property with a broker yet she would not let him show it. After the divorce settlement in which she did not get the house she was so angry that she trashed the home, had the fireplace mantle pulled off the living room wall, took chandeliers, destroyed the property beyond recognition and even pulled trees and shrubs out of the garden. Since the marriage was less than one year, I gave her a lump sum settlement of $100,000 and $2600 a month child support. One would think that with this kind of behavior, I would surely have realized that this woman definitely had a mental problem that I was not capable of dealing with. I cared about the child and kept thinking that Tish was the victim of her childhood deprivation and that all she needed was someone she felt cared about her unconditionally. Over the years I tried to establish a reasonable relationship with her. I helped her a great deal, with child support payment, paid school and other expenses in addition and even let them live with me in my Century City townhouse not only to help them but so I could be with Shane and Torgen, both wonderful little boys. There was no romance or personal relationship between us but soon her possessiveness kicked in and she became jealous of my every move.

I had done a nasal reconstruction on one of the girls in my office. She had a little excess bleeding after the surgery and since she lived in the valley a good distance from the office. I elected to take her home with me so she could sleep on the living room couch for the night and we could take care of her. Here she was with a nose stuffed full of bloody gauze and a splint on her nose with swelling and pain. I had no idea that any woman especially a mother would not have welcomed this opportunity to help some young person just for one night. Tish became violently angry and said, " What do you mean bringing this 'slut' home with you to sleep here?" I said, "Tish she's not a bad person, she's one of my employees. You make it sound like I brought her home for some sex reason and that I am going to allow her to sleep with me. Look at her. Does she look very sexy to you?" She then said, "Get her out of here." With this outrageous behavior, I became angry. I said, "Tish, this is my home and I am allowing you and the boys to stay here because you can't afford your own place. This young lady is sleeping on the couch here whether you like it or not!" With that she picked up one of the fireplaces pokers, came at me and threatened to hit me over the head with it. I pushed her away to avoid the blow, and then she claimed I hit her and went to the phone and called the police and told them I was beating her. Seems I saw this movie before. Two police arrived at the townhouse in a very short time and started to arrest me. I explained to them what had happened, showed them the patient, and told them I did not strike her. They called for a policewoman who examined Tish in the bathroom and found no evidence of injury. They believed me and didn't take me to jail. I had my secretary come and take this poor girl home with her. The patient had witnessed this whole ugly episode and was only too happy to leave my house. After this, I had to get a court order to get Tish out of my home. She moved to Palm Springs where the soap opera continued.

Tish is very smart and has a natural talent for legal matters. She seems to enjoy lawyers and their lawsuits. Her ex husband, John Martinson had a serious tax problem after their divorce and she was involved as the "innocent spouse". The IRS claimed she was responsible for the tax debt along with Martinson. Tish took on the IRS and fought them pro bono for ten years all the way to the Supreme Court and finally won. From that time on she has always been involved in some type of litigation. She cultivated attorneys like most people do friends. As a matter of fact with her feminine charm and good looks she makes "useful friends" out of almost every attorney she meets. She has developed some considerable skills in area of negotiating and legal strategy. However, she seems to always drive a tough bargain and frequently in the end looses by not compromising and taking a little less and letting the deal close. She enjoys the fight and winning is her narcotic.

Tish wrecked two cars of mine: the first was Rolls Royce and the second was Jaguar. Both were beyond repair. This was ten or fifteen years ago and my auto insurance still has a rider that denied coverage if she drives one of my cars.

I bought a big house at Thunderbird Country Club 1993 for spec. I had Tish do the improvements and planned to spend no more than $75,000. By the time she was finished she had spent over $800,000 most of it came from my 401K retirement plan leaving me totally without any retirement funds. This was very stupid on my part but we were so convinced that we would make a big profit on the investment that I allowed her to go way over budget. Tish milked the project over and over: charging personal things to the house such as gardening, maid service, repairs. There was some water damage to the house and she claimed some of her personal furnishings were in the garage and were damaged. She collected from my Insurance Company. Several thousand dollars worth of expensive rugs were charged to the project as carpeting and she took the rugs. Furniture was charged to me on one of those long term one or two year delayed payment without my knowing it until the time was up. All fancy moveable mirrors were charged as built in glasswork.

That was one of the worst depressions in the real estate market. We could not sell this beautiful house for any price in over two years. Our agreement written in our contract was that we both had to agree on the selling price. She set the price at $2.5 million and would not let me lower the price. The only offer we got was $900,000 that was less than the mortgage but Tish wouldn't even allow that. I couldn't keep making the mortgage payments so I lost the house to foreclose and bankruptcy. My attorney advised me to sue Tish to break our contract but it didn't do any good because there were no buyers. So much for my pension and the marriage. For the last year of ownership I moved into the house with Snuffie Adams and at least got the benefit of living in it for at least some of the time. The deal with Tish was that she would furnish the house with her expensive furniture and antiques. When she saw the project was a total failure she moved all of the furniture, hers and mine out in one twenty four hour period.

When I closed my practice in Los Angeles and gave up our Surgery Center (Aesthetica) in 1996 I was still married to Tish. She helped me move all of my valuable artwork and furniture to Palm Springs. She worked very hard and helped the movers because she had a reason. This was a pattern that she repeated three times. The scam was that she would help with the move then generously suggest that most of the valuable items to be stored at her large home in Rancho Mirage. This seemed like a good idea. It would save me some storage expense. However once these items entered her house they became her property. I was never allowed to retrieve anything. Her mantra was: "possession is nine tenths of the law". She did it again when I moved from the Bel Air house on Buckingham Lane.

By the year 2000 I had retrieved some wealth through Inamed Corp., the breast implant maker. I married for the sixth time to Snuffie Adams and bought a home in Bel Air Crest. After the divorce from Snuffie, she moved out with all of her "belongings" then I allowed Tish and Shane, my teenager son, to live there with me for a short time. When the house was sold Tish offered to help me move my things (I never learn) and repeated the exact scenario. Moving some of the valuable things to her house never to be mine again.

When I put the house up for sale it was with a broker at Caldwell Banker by the name of Sam. Since the house was in Snuffie's name she negotiated the deal at the standard commission of 6%. Sam found a buyer right away but I wouldn't sign off on the sale because the divorce settlement had not been completed. By the time I was ready to sell Tish was involved and she wanted me to offer Sam only 4% commission or lose the listing. He had already found a buyer once and felt that he deserved the listing at the standard 6%. I then found another broker who would take the listing at 4%. At that time the IRS was after me to pay taxes on the "Phantom Income" generated from the sale of my Inamed stock. I had hoped I could make the sale before they could levy on the property. Somehow Sam found out about the tax problem and in his anger reported the impending sale to the IRS. They immediately put a lien on the property but allowed the sale to go through because they would rather levy the cash equity than the house. Some time before, I had put the property in a Nevada Corp. and signed over all of the stock ownership to Tish. I chose Tish because she was the one who would have to see Shane, the 18 year old, through high school and College. Our attorney, Bob Kluger, drafted a "Buyout Agreement" that would call for Tish to receive $300,000 of the $600,000 equity and I would have no more responsibility for child support. The IRS "Pierced the Corporate Vail". They claimed that the Nevada Corp and I were the same. Tish, with her own attorney, filed a lawsuit against the IRS over ownership of the Nevada Corp. The funds were placed in a joint account until the court could settle the issue. Even before the court hearing on the matter the IRS took the money (now with interest the amount in the bank account was around $650,000.) The court ruling was a summery judgment in favor of the government.

During this time Tish was in the process of refinancing her home in Rancho Mirage and could not make the mortgage payments. Because she was heavily involved in the fight with the IRS and I didn't want to see her lose her home and the home of my son I advanced her a total of $70,000 over the period of one year so she could make those payments. She claimed the money was to pay her attorneys but it was not.

She had promised to repay me when her new home loan was funded. Her scam was that is she could earmark the funds for attorneys she would not have to repay me. That's what she did. In order to qualify for her home loan she had to show that she had funds in a bank account. She had her attorney form a trust with me as Trustor and her as the Beneficiary. The deal was that I put $ 25,000 in her Trust bank account that would show on her statement and when the new mortgage was funded I was to get every dollar of my money back. The trust agreement clearly stated that there could be none of the funds taken out without my written approval. Next thing I knew all of the money was gone from the Trust and its bank account was closed. The attorney had taken most of it for legal fees and Tish took the remainder. Tish claimed she had nothing to do with it and the attorney claimed she gave him permission to deplete the Trust.

Chapter Twenty Seven

Snuffie

SNUFFIE AND ME

IT WAS IN 1974 that I decided to open the branch office in Palm Springs. I had bought a Condominium at the Springs but I could never get my wife, Shannon to come down even for a weekend. My schedule was to drive down after dinner on Wednesday, arrive around 10 o'clock, early to bed and rest up for the surgery that was scheduled for Thursday and Friday. I would spend the weekend and make house calls to see the patients on Saturday then return to Los Angeles on Sunday. This worked so well that I decided to open a new office there. I found the perfect space in a new office building called One Hawkeye Park in Rancho Mirage. It just so happened that the famous interior designer, Steve Chase had his offices in the same complex. I had admired his work and decided to have him and his staff do my new office.

There was a flood in the Condo when the hot water line to the washer-drier broke. I asked Snuffie Adams who worked with Steve to manage the renovation and redecorating. I got to know her and we started a relationship that lasted for years. We were on again and off again over the time both having other relationships. I even got married to another woman, Tish and had a son, Shane. After the divorce from Tish, Snuffie and I got together again and lived together for almost five years. It was very happy times for me with Snuffie. She was the wife I was looking for: a near perfect relationship without marriage. She was a joy.

During this time I was trying to get along with ex-wife Tish so I did a joint venture with her on a spec house at the Thunderbird Country Club. We had a contract that gave her control of the selling price. We invested way too much money at one of the worst times in the real estate business. The house was on the market for over three years and never sold. In order to get some value or use of the house I moved in with Snuffie. This was a beautiful home; why not enjoy it as long as we can? I had never been happier, living now with a reasonable and normal lady that's been there for me for so many years. She is kind, overly generous and a total joy to be with. She even loves the game of golf as I do.

I knew there had to be a woman like this somewhere but my "trial and error" method had not worked in five tries. I had known Snuffie for almost twenty years and lived with her for five of those years.

SNUFFIE'S FAMILY

Snuffie had two beautiful daughters, Ami and Allison. They both married great men that were the best, handsome, intelligent and very successful. They are the perfect little families. Ami (Settlemier) has three sons with Reid: Brock, Trent and Spencer. Allison (Bollen) has a son and a daughter; Blake and Brook with John.

The Settlemiers own an interesting company, (Biggie) that sells and rents huge cranes all over the world. John Bollen is a Tech genius that is in the process of over-seeing the electronic marvels of a multi billion-dollar hotel construction in Las Vegas.

SNUFFIE & DAUGHTERS

On September 11th the World Trade Center in New York was destroyed by insane Terrorists who flew hijacked American and United Airlines planes, full of innocent people into the magnificent twin towers and the Pentagon. Snuffie's birthday was on the tenth one-day earlier. On that day we had just returned from a week trip to Nassau where we visited some friends. We both thought we knew the other as well as you could know anyone. We were married on April 20, 2000 after having lived together for over six years. It was a happy occasion because we both believe we had given our relationship plenty of time to know it had a good chance to be lasting.

Married a year and it was wonderful. It was full of love, generosity, and happiness. We never had a problem or a fight. We bought a beautiful home in Bel Air Crest, California and Snuffle kept her small house in Palm Springs. Both homes were in her name as her sole and separate property.

Due to a bankruptcy in 1996 I could not qualify for the mortgage so I made a gift to her for $600,000 as the down payment. Of course Snuffie considered this a gift of love. This was a sweet thought but she knew it was really a gift of necessity, the only way we could buy the house. Our premarital agreement stated that after our marriage the house would convert to community property.

Snuffie does Interior Designer and is an extreme perfectionist. She runs her life like it is one of her decorating jobs. Every thing has to be perfect at all times. She has "rules" that have to be adhered to without question. Never leave a dirty dish out of the dishwasher. Clothing always either hung up of in the laundry bag. She then checks it and makes any slight adjustments in the pillow arrangement if they don't look perfect to her. Sometimes I will move a small accessory on a table, then time her to see how long it would take before she comes along and puts it back in it's original position. The time is measured in minutes or seconds.

One day I learned how important her clothes were to her and that her closets were "sacred" ground never to be violated or even entered by others and specially me, the husband. My young son, Shane had an event at his school. The theme was to come to the school that day dressed like some character from the movies. He and friend decided to dress like "Men in black" a Will Smith flick. This of course required them to wear black suits and dark glasses that Shane did not have. It was the middle of the day and Snuffle was not home. I naively thought that perhaps I might find something suitable in her massive collection of clothes. Voila! I found this beautiful black coat that, with the aid of a few safety pins, fit him just fine. The dark glasses were no problem so the kid had a wonderful day and he and his friend won the prize for the best idea. At the end of the day we got the black suit back to Snuffle's closet but she caught us. We had committed the mortal sin by violating the "sanctity" of her wardrobe. How could I possibly have done such a thing? Let this thirteen-year-old kid wear one of her most expensive outfits and possibly ruin it. It was as though we deserved capital punishment. We examined the suit carefully and found no damage and I even offered to buy her another one if there had been. It didn't matter we were busted!

Speaking of closets: In Snuffle's small Palm Springs house there is a limited amount of space to hang one's clothes because it is one of the older homes around Canyon Country Club. In the days when this house was built people didn't seem to need as much closet space. They didn't have such large wardrobes like my dear Snuffle has. Her clothes collection is massive but nothing compared to one of her friends who's rich husband built a closet addition to their bedroom measuring over 10,000 square feet. Knowing this makes Snuffle think she doesn't have any clothes at all. At any rate my share of the space is less than 2%.

Snuffie's extreme obsessive-compulsive perfectionism does not apply only to her physical environment but also the way she manages her life. She loves to give orders and have them carried out immediately. If a man is told what to do all the time and he wants a peaceful relationship he is likely to stop thinking for himself and surrenders to his wife, letting her "run his life." If he lets this happen then he will gradually become a "Casper Milk-Toast" and lose his confidence in himself and his self-esteem. In turn the wife will gradually lose respect for him and he will become a nonentity in her life. She might then start looking for a "Real Man" who will tell her what to do with her life. I believe this is what most women want but will not admit it. To exercise power and control over any other person's life is destructive. (This is my theory. I could be wrong).

Over the six years before our marriage Snuffle and I lived together, first in the big Thunderbird home until it was lost to foreclosure, then in her small home on Alhambra Drive in Palm Springs. I love Snuffie. She has great talent and creativity and is most generous. The five grandchildren are her life. Every time she visits them it's like Christmas. She takes them so many gifts that they have come to expect it every time "Mimi" shows up. It's none of my business I know and she would be the first to let me know that. She's a fabulous grandmother and her love for those wonderful children is boundless.

Early in 2002 Snuffie was taking some hormone replacement therapy and I was on some Testosterone. We both noticed that we were more aggressive than normal and had a little dispute while dining at Mamma Gina Restaurant. It grew out of proportion resulting in me calling her an obsessive-compulsive bitch. She ordered me out of her house on January 17, 2002 and divorced me after less than two years of marriage. (There is no room for error here.)

On July 22, 2004 Snuffie's girl friend Rosemary made an appointment and came to my office to reveal that Snuffie wanted to rekindle a relationship with me. This was very good news to me because I had never stopped loving and caring for Snuffie. We have not remarried because that seems to be where the trouble comes from. The marital contract seems to change everything. It's better when the door swings both ways. That way no one is trapped and the lawyers are, for the most part, kept out of our lives. For three years now we have spent as much time together as we can and are very happy.

In the latter part of August, 2006 I was diagnosed as having a leak in one of my heart valves and was scheduled for surgery at St.Johns Hospital in Santa Monica, California on September 11, the anniversary of the New York disaster. It wasn't planned but I don't think I will have much trouble remembering the date. Snuffie was my Florence Nightingale, the best caretaker and nurse one could possible find. I am so lucky to have her in my life.

My children were notified and they all came to see me in the hospital. I love their response. I would have the surgery again just to get them together. It seems it takes a heart operation to justify a family reunion. I used to have a traditional Christmas dinner every year at the Bel Air Country club for the whole family but after the first two, some of them voted against the idea. I was never sure why.

My heart surgeon, Dr. John Roberts said I went through the open-heart surgery like a 45year old.

On March 24 1998 I wrote the following letter to all my patients:

⌒

RETIREMENT LETTER ONE

JOHN E WILLIAMS, M.D.

Dear Patient,   March 24, 1998

This letter is to inform you that I have retired from active practice of Plastic Surgery. It is with regret that I do this because I have always enjoyed the work and especially my patients. I have been fortunate to be able to practice for over fifty years.

It is now time to turn my scalpel over to younger hands and I have chosen the best pair of younger hands that I have ever encountered. Equally important is what goes along with this skill. Dr Garth Fisher is a charming, attractive and caring doctor. His first entry into practice was in our Century City Office when he finished his excellent training. I have seen him grow and develop into one of the most outstanding plastic surgeons in California. I am proud to recommend him for further care and treatment of my patients.

It has been a real pleasure having you as a patient and I want to thank you for allowing me that privilege.

Thank you again for allowing me to help you where I could.

Sincerely yours,

John E. Williams, M.D.

⌒

RETIREMENT LETTER TWO
John Williams, M.D.

Dear Friends and Former Patients   March 25, 2000

A couple of years ago I decided to retire from the practice of Plastic Surgery. It was a bad idea. Like most people, I bought into the idea that "retirement" was the ultimate goal to work for that allows you to spend the rest of your life doing only pleasurable activities. It's boring and a waste of talent. I miss the work and especially my wonderful patients. I can still do the work as well as ever and I have kept up with the amazing innovations and improvement in techniques that continue to evolve. With the use of lasers, endoscopes, and better instruments the trend has been in making the procedures less invasive and easier on the patient. The one operation that has gone the other way by making the procedure progressively more complicated and requiring more time and risk is the face-lift. I am excited about a relatively new procedure that can be done in less than half the time and allow the patient to be up and about in as little as three days.

If you would like to recapture a more youthful appearance this could be the best time to do it.

I will be sharing offices with Dr. Ray Henderson and can be contacted for consultations at:

73-180 El Paseo
Palm Desert, California 92260
760 -346-3810

Sincerely,
John Williams, M.D

As explained in the second letter, I hated retirement. I gave up the L.A. office in April 1998 but continued to do surgery in Dr. Monroe Sternlieb's surgical center in Rancho Mirage.

I have found it very difficult to retire for several reasons. I love the profession of Plastic Surgery and as long as I can do the surgery skillfully and safely for the patient I like to continue doing it. I'm told that in Canada the hospitals suspend their doctor's privileges when they reach the age of sixty-five. Today with the increased longevity and prolonged good heath that is a massive waste of talent. Many doctors are at their best from sixty-five to seventy five. What a waist. The gratitude of the patients is my main compensation. Recently I had a 24-year-old man show up at my office, having traveled all the way from Australia to thank me for repairing his harelip when he was born. That is my joy and pleasure in doing this work.

Chapter Twenty Eight

Inamed Corporation

DON MCGHAN THE founder of Inamed Corporation appointed me to the board in 1997. Being on the board of directors of a corporation was a whole new world for me. I found it fascinating and enjoyed it very much. McGhan Medical Corp. is a medium size company that makes breast implant and other medical devices. They were heavily involved in the silicone breast class action lawsuit and were lucky to have survived it. My friend Don McGhan, the founder of the company had a lot of problems with the settlement of the lawsuit and some Securities and Exchange Commission issues. He was looking for some one who qualified to be the CEO of the company. He and the Directors had considered several people but no one seemed to fit or qualify for the job. My long time friend Dick Babbitt had retired and was living in the desert. Playing golf every day was his passion but it didn't fulfill his life. He had owned and run several companies of his own and had a great resume. I had told him to get back to work because he was bored and had too much corporate talent to waste it on the golf course. I asked him if he would be interested in the job with Inamed and he said he would. I submitted his resume to the board and they tabled it because they were negotiating with another party. This fell through so I submitted his resume again and he was hired.

The original McGhan Medical Corporation was incorporated in

1974 and was a manufacturer of silicone implants products for plastic and reconstructive surgery. In 1977 the business was sold to Minnesota Mining and Manufacturing Company (3M). The 3M company didn't know what to do with this medical device company so in 1984 Don McGhan formed a new McGhan Medical Corporation and acquired the assets of 3M's silicone implant product line. In 1985 this entity became a subsidiary of a public company through a merger with First American Corporation, a Florida corporation. In 1986 First American Corporation changed its name to Inamed Corporation. In December 1998, Inamed changed it state of incorporation to Delaware.

On January 23, 1998 Dick Babbitt was hired as President and Chief Executive Officer, and Ilan K. Reich as Executive Vice President. I had been on the board of directors since March 31, 1997.

In 1992, the FDA declared a moratorium on silicone gel-filled implants because of claims that these implants caused connective tissue disease. This generated a tide of litigation against all U.S. breast manufactures including Inamed subsidiaries McGhan Medical. Between 1992 and 1998 the company was named as a defendant or co-defendant in thousands of lawsuits and other claims.

On June 2, 1998, federal Judge Sam C. Pointer, Jr. gave preliminary approval of the settlement agreement with the plaintiffs' class settlement lawyers. Under these agreements, Inamed agreed to pay an aggregate of $31.5 million. Inamed's major competitor, Mentor had settled earlier and paid something around $25.0 million.

There has never been any medical or scientific evidence that silicone gel caused any of the claimed diseases. The total amount of all the claims is estimated to be around $54.0 billion. What a bonanza for the lawyers.

Dick Babbitt did a great job of running Inamed and solving most of it's challenging problems even though he was ruthless in dealing with the McGhan family he made them wealthier. The domestic or U.S. Company remained under the name of McGhan Medical. This was the main production of saline filled breast implants. He restructured the international companies from 25 independent subsidiaries to one. The third division was the Lap Band device company manufacturing and marketing obesity devices. During my time with the company the stock went from a low of around $2.50 to $48.00 a share and has doubled since. Dick had accumulated over 250,000 shares (more later). He turned the company over to new senior management in 2004 and retired back to the golf (Bel Air Country Club) he loved. He died there on the seventeenth green in July 2005. If he had to die he would not have chosen a better place.

EPILOGUE

DR. JIM CONTINUED to practice for about two years after moving back to Cookeville Tennessee, Lavenia's hometown. He had suffered with heart rhythm problems (atrial fibrillation) for some time and had required 8 or 9 shock treatments in attempt to convert his heart rate to normal sinus rhythm. During the fibrillation, clots can form in the heart, break loose and go to the brain causing a stroke. This is what happened to Jim. He had a mild stroke that left him with weakness on his left side. Medication such as Coumadin or Aspirin is usually taken in attempt to prevent this from happening. This combined with the accident in which he ran over his own leg in a car he was driving (chapter 23) significantly affected his general health. He had agonizing complications after having open-heart surgery that resulted in his death on March 10, 2003. He was a major part of my life that has continued now four years beyond his and I still enjoy good health. I wonder why? I am grateful to have had him for a life partner in every thing I have done except my six marriages. He takes no blame for that. He was a kind, honest, gentleman, a talented surgeon and inventor, an excellent husband and father. He loved life, enjoyed hunting and fishing. He was spiritual and embraced religion with his loving wife, Lavenia. I loved him and I miss him.

Appendix I

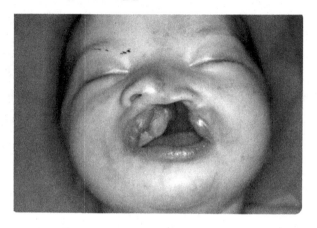

PREOPERATIVE VIEW,
WIDE COMPLETE CLEFT LIP AND PALATE.

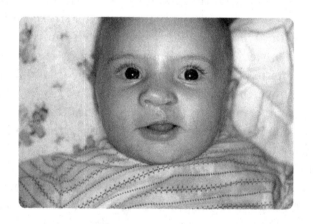

POSTOPERATIVE VIEW,
AGE FOUR MONTHS, PRIMARY CHEILOPLASTY,
' MILLARD PROCEDURE'

Appendix II

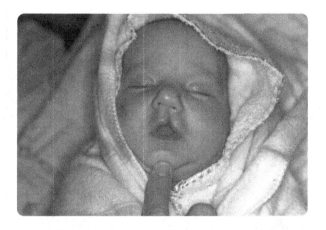

PREOPERATIVE VIEW,
UNILATERAL INCOMPLETE CLEFT LIP.

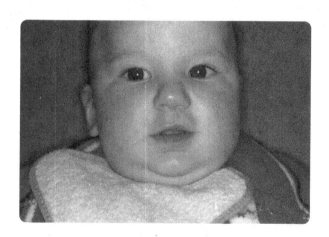

POSTOPERATIVE VIEW,
FIVE MONTHS, PRIMARY CHEILOPLASTY
'MILLARD PROCEDURE'.

Appendix III

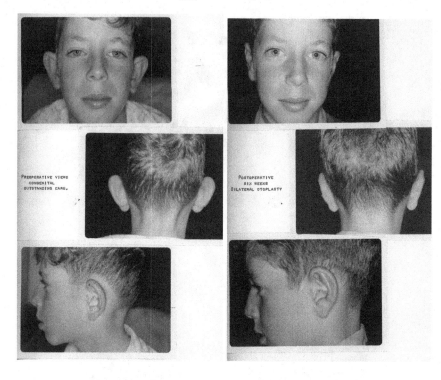

PREOPERATIVE VIEWS
CONGENITAL
OUTSTANDING EARS.

POSTOPERATIVE
SIX WEEKS
BILATERAL OTOPLASTY

Appendix IV

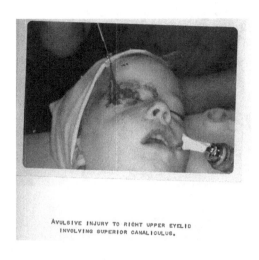

AVULSIVE INJURY TO RIGHT UPPER EYELID
INVOLVING SUPERIOR CANALICULUS.

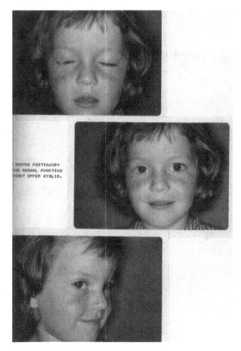

MONTHS POSTINJURY
NORMAL FUNCTION
RIGHT UPPER EYELID.

Appendix V

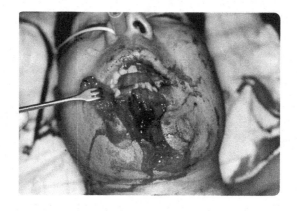

COMPOUND FRACTURE OF MANDIBLE
WITH FULL THICKNESS LACERATION
OF CHIN AND LOWER LIP EXTENDING
INTO FLOOR OF MOUTH RESULTING
FROM AN AUTOMOBILE ACCIDENT.

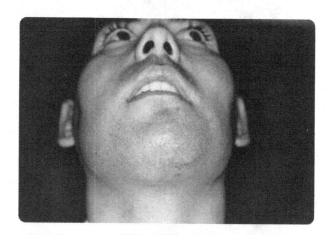

ABOVE: THREE MONTHS AFTER INJURY,
SCAR ON CHIN TO BE REVISED.

BELOW: SHOWS SOME LINGUAL ROTATION
OF RIGHT SIDE OF MANDIBLE
DUE TO BONE LOSS.

Appendix VI

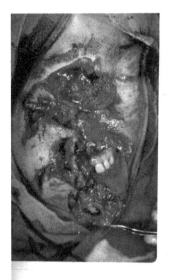 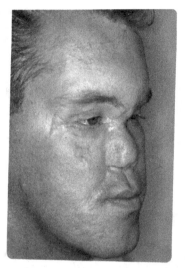

LEFT VIEW SHOWS THE INJURY WITH RIGHT EYE
DISPLACED LATERALLY. RIGHT HALF OF MAXILLARY
ALVEOLUS AND TEETH WERE FOUND IN PATIENTS CAR.
REMNENT OF LEFT NASAL PASSAGE RETRACTED WITH
FORCEPS, WAS REPAIRABLE.

RIGHT VIEW, FACIAL REPAIR APPROXIMATELY 6 MONTHS
AFTER BONE GRAFT BENEATH RIGHT EYE.

Appendix VII

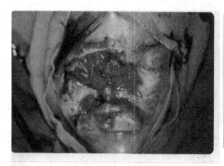

25 YEAR OLD MALE WITH EXTENSIVE FACIAL
INJURY DUE TO AUTO ACCIDENT.

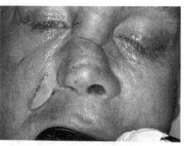

FLAP AT UPPER NASAL DORSUM WELL
HEALED AND SOFTENING.

NASO-LABIAL FOLD FLAP DESIGNED TO
REPLACE MISSING RIGHT ALAR BASE.

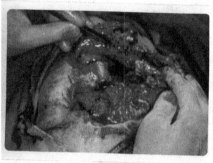

ENTIRE RIGHT MAXILLA DESTROYED INCLUDING ORBITAL FLOOR
AND ALVEOLUS. RIGHT NASAL PASSAGE OBLITERATED. NOTE
NASAL TIP AND UPPER LIP ATTACHED ONLY BY SMALL
PEDICLE AT RIGHT COMMISSURE.

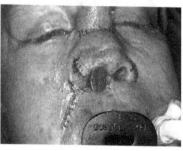

IMMEDIATE POSTOPERATIVE VIEW OF
RECONSTRUCTED RIGHT ALAR BASE.
LOWER END OF NASAL BRIDGE FLAP
REVISED. SKIN GRAFT IN PLACE TO
RELINE NASAL PASSAGE.

Above Patient Appendix Vi, Vii

John Norris, age 25, white male
OCCUPATION: Laborer
HOSPITAL: Gardena Hospital, Inc., Gardena, California
HOSPITAL NUMBER: 57308
DATE ADMITTED: October 9, 1961
DATES OF SURGERY: During the first admission, October 9, 1961,
                         October 21, 1961°
DATE DISCHARGED: December 4, 1961
ADMITTING DIAGNOSIS: Extensive facial injury, shock, and possible craneo-cerebral injury.

HISTORY

Patient a 25 year old, white male was involved in at automobile accident on October 9, 1961, when he fell asleep at the wheel and ran into a scaffolding that was being used for the construction of a freeway. The patient sustained a severe facial injury when a 4" x 6" timber crashed through the windshield and into his face. Patient was brought to the Emergency Room of the Gardena Hospital immediately. Upon arrival he was unconscious and in shock with a blood pressure of 80/40. In the Emergency Room, an intravenous was started with 500 cc of dextran. Patient was typed and cross-matched for blood and a tracheostomy performed in the Emergency Room. The massive open wounds of the face were packed with sterile gauze and a pressure dressing applied to control bleeding. He was then taken to operating room.

The above is the medical history when John Norris was first seen in the emergency room with this massive facial injury. This was a major challenge and I spent over eight hours in the O.R. repairing this face. How do you begin one might ask? The answer to that is: the deep structures (anatomy) that were recognizable. Then repair them all the way to the skin. The right eye was hanging by the optic nerve. The upper dental arch was so free in the wound it looked like a false denture. Fortunately the blood supply in the mid face is excellent and the bone structures are fairly delicate so it withstands severe trauma. If this injury had have been a few inches higher and struck his forehead it would have killed him.

As the photos show, many reconstructive procedures were required. I spent so much time with Norris he became my surrogate son. He kept asking me why I didn't let him die. He called me to tell me about everything in his life. He was arrested for drunk driving and I bailed him out of jail. As he began to look a bit more human his life improved. He got married. He told me that he did it just to see if he could. He went on to father a child and then began making those frequent calls to thank me for saving his face and his life.

Appendix VIII

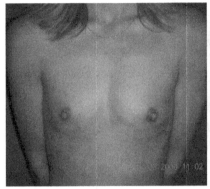 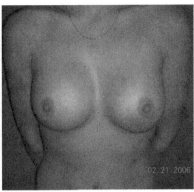

BEFORE   AFTER

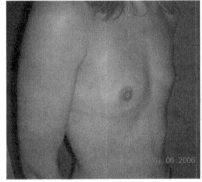 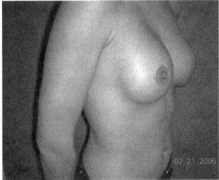

BEFORE   AFTER

BREAST IMPLANTS

Appendix IX

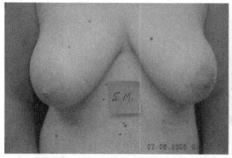 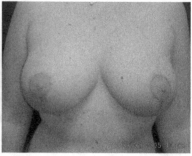

BEFORE   AFTER

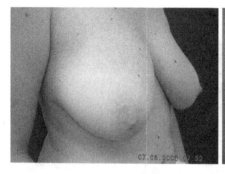 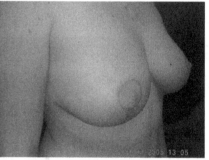

BEFORE   AFTER

BREAST REDUCTION

Appendix X

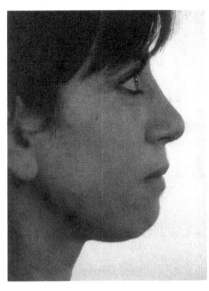 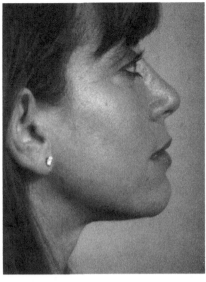

BEFORE   AFTER

NOSE AND CHIN

Appendix XI

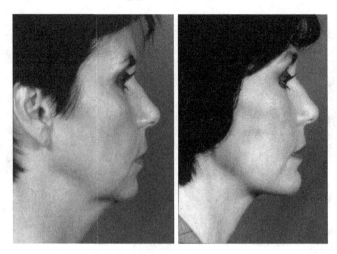

BEFORE   AFTER

FACE LIFT AND CHIN IMPLANT

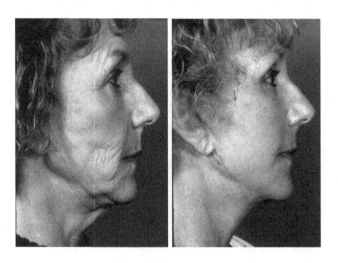

BEFORE   AFTER

FACE LIFT

Appendix XII

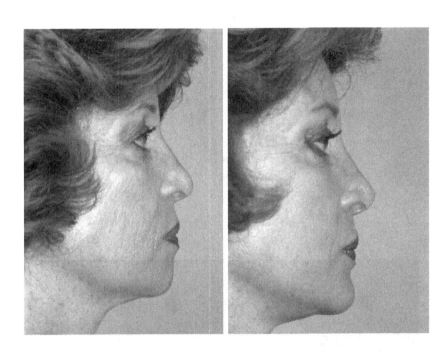

BEFORE   AFTER

CHIN IMPLANT

Appendix XIII

RHINOPLASTY

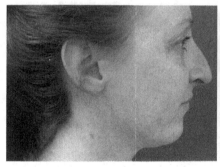 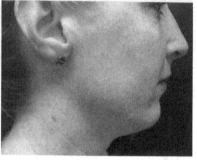

BEFORE   AFTER

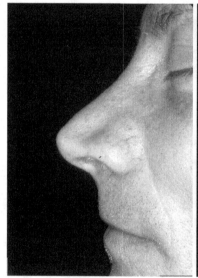 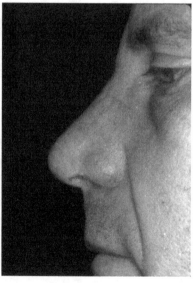

BEFORE   AFTER

Printed in the United States
By Bookmasters